Virtual Local Manufacturing Communities

Virtual Local Manufacturing Communities

Online Simulations of Future Workshop Systems

William Sims Bainbridge

BEP BUSINESS EXPERT PRESS

Virtual Local Manufacturing Communities: Online Simulations of Future Workshop Systems

First published in 2019 by
Business Expert Press, LLC
222 East 46th Street, New York, NY 10017
www.businessexpertpress.com

ISBN-13: 978-1-94858-074-8 (paperback)
ISBN-13: 978-1-94858-073-1 (e-book)

Business Expert Press Collaborative Intelligence Collection

Cover and interior design by Exeter Premedia Services Private Ltd., Chennai, India

First edition: 2019

10 9 8 7 6 5 4 3 2 1

Printed in the United States of America.

Abstract

Distributed manufacturing offers the promise of bringing jobs back to local communities, producing goods that are personalized or harmonize with distinctive cultures, and thereby reversing significant aspects of the globalization that has dominated in recent years. Large corporations may still have important roles to play, but in collaboration with local workshops, for example providing machinery, software, databases of designs, and communication media suitable for a diverse and dynamic workforce. For two decades a largely unrecognized set of computer simulation laboratories has flourished, in which millions of people have used virtual machines to produce a great variety of products: massively multiplayer online role-playing games. Their systems are highly diverse, often complex, and provide information capable of serious social science analysis. This book deeply explores 30 of these production-capable social media, based on thousands of hours of observation and extensive collection of statistical data, extracting hypotheses that may generalize to the real-world distributed manufacturing of the near future. This book begins with an overview of this universe of online virtual worlds then demonstrates the principles of virtual manufacturing, modes of work-related communication, socio-economic structures and dynamics, and the function of artificial intelligence in these human-technology systems. It concludes with consideration of the large-scale technical and cultural variation illustrated both by individual examples and by the rather large industry in which they have long been successful.

Keywords

3-D printing; artificial intelligence; avatar; computer simulation; community; distributed manufacture; globalization; human–computer interaction; multiplayer games; rapid prototyping; role-playing; social media; virtual world

Contents

CHAPTER 1

Virtual Exploration of Real Possibilities

Computer-controlled manufacturing technologies, combined with information technologies capable of supporting new forms of social organization, have the potential to take humanity far beyond the industrial revolution, to an economy in which many products of value in daily life are produced again locally in small workshops. Large corporations will still be significant but playing somewhat different roles. They will provide much of the machinery used in local manufacturing, the computer-aided design software used to personalize each product, and the communication systems that support cooperation between people and technologies. It seems likely that some categories of products will be suitable for a franchise system, in which a multinational corporation will set standards and provide methods, working through legally established relationships with a system of locally owned workshops. Imagination can explore a variety of possibilities, but for the past two decades a virtual online experiment has taken place from which insights and ideas may be derived: massively multiplayer online role-playing games.

Over four decades ago, a leading innovator of information technology advocated the use of advanced electronic communication systems to support the return of population from the cities of the industrial era to towns and villages. His name was Peter Goldmark, and he was largely responsible for the development of long-playing phonographs and had contributed to the development of color television. After retirement from CBS laboratories in 1971, Wikipedia reports,

> he pursued research on the use of communication technologies to provide services like teleconferencing and remote medical consultations to people in rural areas. Funded by the U.S. National

Science Foundation in the early 1970s, the "New Rural Society Project" was housed at Fairfield University in Fairfield, Conn., and conducted pilot studies across the state in Eastern Connecticut's relatively rural Windham region.[1]

The National Science Foundation's (NSF) online grant database does not confirm its support, and another source implies that it may have been a small contribution within "generous funding from the federal Departments of Housing and Urban Development (over $700,000) and the Transportation ($150,000) and the National Science Foundation."[2]

In a 1972 *Scientific American* article predicting the development of today's networked society, Goldmark noted, "Cities exist largely because they enhance communications."[3] In a cascade of speeches and even in the *Congressional Record*, he argued that large cities waste energy, notably through daily commuting to and from work, and that they promote crime and disintegrate social relationships.[4] Were he alive today, he would rejoice in the widespread adoption of Internet, complain that society had failed to rebuild local communities, and quite possibly suggest that multiplayer online games were valuable simulations of the future he hoped would come.

Whether abbreviated MMORPG, or more efficiently if imprecisely MMO, massively multiplayer online role-playing games attracted millions of players and billions of dollars to play activities that focused on adventure stories and simulated combat. But in the background of most popular examples was a virtual economy incorporating simulated gathering of raw materials and production of valuable goods. These were not limited to medieval-style weapons and body armor, but included foods,

---

[1] en.wikipedia.org/wiki/Peter_Carl_Goldmark

[2] Freeze, K.J., and P.C. Goldmark. 2001. "Technological Visionary." Presented at the IEEE Conference on the History of Telecommunications, Memorial University, St. John's, Newfoundland, p. 7, July 25–27. ethw.org/w/images/0/0d/Freeze.pdf

[3] Goldmark, P.C. September 1972. "Communication and the Community." *Scientific American* 227, no. 3, pp. 142–51.

[4] "Dr. Goldmark on a New Rural Society." July 8, 1974. *Congressional Record—Senate*, pp. 22257–59.

fashionable clothing, transportation vehicles, and even houses and the furniture to fill them. Often, players bought and sold such manufactured items through an in-game marketplace or traded them among groups of friends. MMOs are persistent worlds, the oldest one analyzed here having flourished for over 20 years, and players were encouraged to create enduring social groups, typically called *guilds*, which perhaps not coincidentally was the name for professional societies in the decades prior to the industrial revolution. In April 2008, the author of this book created a guild named Science specifically to hold a scientific conference in *World of Warcraft*, the most popular MMO which had about 12,000,000 subscribers, at which 120 academics discussed the significance of virtual worlds, leading to publication of a conventional book on that topic.[5] At the time of the last report, that guild was still active although no longer serving research functions, thus one example of how virtual social systems can endure and evolve.

On the basis of intensive study of 30 MMOs, this book will explore several dimensions of online simulation of local production. Although not designed by academics to test scientific theories, they serve as intellectually rich simulations, all the more informative because they were designed by smart, technologically sophisticated enthusiasts who not only had their own ideas about human cooperation, but also learned from each other and from the players who responded with varying levels of enthusiasm to the designers' innovations. Many academic studies have found real merit in research on MMOs, identifying many connections to real-world socioeconomic systems.[6] Using Jay Forester's academic simulations of cities as his classical example, Matthew Wells has argued that even seriously intended academic computer models blur the distinction between fact and fiction and that many of the more complex computer games should be taken seriously.[7]

[5] Bainbridge, W.S., ed. 2010. *Online Worlds: Convergence of the Real and the Virtual*. London: Springer.

[6] Lakkaraju, K., G. Sukthankar, and R.T. Wigand. 2018. *Social Interaction in Virtual Worlds*. Cambridge University Press. Add more.

[7] Wells, M. 2016. "Deliberate Constructions of the Mind: Simulation Games as Fictional Models." *Games and Culture* 11, no. 5, pp. 528–47.

Much of the research effort invested to date in small-scale distributed manufacturing has employed the conceptualization of the maker movement and focused on its educational potential, whereas also suggesting that very practical benefits could result. Wikipedia describes this movement as "a contemporary culture or subculture representing a technology-based extension of DIY culture."[8] "Literally meaning 'do it yourself,' the DIY ethic promotes the idea that anyone is capable of performing a variety of tasks rather than relying on paid specialists."[9] However, the long-term result is likely to be a workforce collaborating along a spectrum from amateur to professional, not "do it yourself" but "do it ourselves."

For example, a June 12, 2015, press release of the NSF was titled "New paths to innovation and learning through DIY technologies" and announced:

> Today, the nation of makers proves it has no borders, as do-it-yourself engineers, inventors and tinkerers of all ages and backgrounds converge at the National Maker Faire. The National Science Foundation (NSF) directly supports many of the exhibitors—known as "makers"—participating in the faire, with even more exhibitors using NSF-funded tools and technologies, such as 3-D printing and computer-aided design. The faire is a kickoff event for the National Week of Making June 12–18, which celebrates the growing wave of innovators enabled by access to new resources and knowledge, known as the maker movement.[10]

A year earlier, an NSF news release titled "Engineering for All" praised the contributions of professionals to the liberation of amateurs:

> Today's engineers are helping to drive many of the technologies that make making possible—from 3-D printers to user-friendly design software. As high fabrication costs and complicated computer programs become a thing of the past, young inventors and

---

[8] en.wikipedia.org/wiki/Maker_culture
[9] en.wikipedia.org/wiki/DIY_ethic
[10] www.nsf.gov/news/news_summ.jsp?cntn_id=135397

DIY (do-it-yourself) enthusiasts can focus on what really matters: bringing their ideas to life.[11]

A prominent method for small-scale manufacture is 3-D printing or *additive manufacture*, originally a form of *rapid prototyping*, that can efficiently produce small numbers of products and change their exact specifications easily. The term "small scale" may be misleading, because a huge amount of effort has been invested in developing these technologies, and if designed and organized well these methods can manufacture large numbers of products, but with highly flexible designs that can be customized for particular users. Already by 2013, the NSF reportedly had made 600 grants totaling $200,000,000 in research on additive manufacture, primarily through its Engineering Directorate.[12] An early example of widespread local manufacturing using additive manufacture is the production of unique assistive technologies, such as artificial hands customized to fit the arms of specific disabled people.[13]

This example is analogous to the virtual production of body armor in historical and fantasy action-oriented online games. Generally, the user is able to customize the avatar, in many cases given the opportunity to set its body size and shape. In making a virtual helmet, it is generally taken for granted that it will fit the already-determined virtual head of the avatar, so customization is generally ignored with respect to its dimensions. However, different classes of avatars are allowed to wear only particular kinds of armor, for example, steel versus leather, which require working with different simulated materials and often at different simulated machines. As is true also for academic research that employs computer simulation, some parts of a dynamic process are represented more precisely than

---

[11] www.nsf.gov/discoveries/disc_summ.jsp?cntn_id=131735

[12] Weber, C., V. Peña, M. Micali, E. Yglesias, S. Rood, J.A. Scott, and B. Lal. 2013. *The Role of the National Science Foundation in the Origin and Evolution of Additive Manufacturing in the United States.* Washington, DC: IDA Science & Technology Policy Institute.

[13] Buehler, E., S. Branham, A. Ali, J.J. Chang, M.K. Hofmann, A. Hurst, and S.K. Kane. 2015." Sharing is Caring: Assistive Technology Designs on Thingiverse." In *Proceedings of CHI 2015*, 525–34. New York, NY: ACM.

others. We can distinguish *explicit simulation*, using algorithms that represent all the processes in realistic detail, from *implicit simulation* in which only the input and output are accurately represented. The commercial online games use a mixture of implicit and explicit, thus rendering some aspects of simulated manufacturing more precise than others.

Additive manufacture is a good example, both because its value for the future economy is clear and because it typically employs computer systems not very different from simulation graphics software to produce its products. But there are at least two other kinds of local manufacture that may be significant in the future: (1) revival of historic workshop production of everyday items like furniture and dishware and (2) creation of community-related information resources. This book emphasizes simulated manufacture of physical objects, but information products are also covered, notably schematics or instructions about how to manufacture physical products.

Arguably, mass production of many durable household items, and also personal clothing, was historically connected with a particular phase in economic growth, beginning well over a century ago.[14] Very prosperous families, however, often filled their homes with antique furniture and their kitchens with distinctive dishes and wore highly customized clothing, at least for formal occasions. If society stabilizes with a significant fraction of the population able to afford goods that are more costly than the absolute minimum, then production of local goods will increase, designed not only to serve the desires of individual customers, but also to harmonize with local cultures.

We can suggest that additive manufacturing can be paired with *subtractive manufacturing*. Computers are quite capable of controlling lathes and wood-carving machinery, for example, to make distinctive legs for a dining table intended to serve its family in their preferred style. Automatic

---

[14] Livesay, H.C., and P.G. Porter. 1969. "Vertical Integration in American Manufacturing, 1899-1948." *The Journal of Economic History* 29, no. 3, pp. 494–500; Lamoreaux, N.R., D.M. Raff, and P. Temin. 2003. "Beyond Markets and Hierarchies: Toward a New Synthesis of American Business History." *The American Historical Review* 108, no. 2, pp. 404–33.

drilling and milling machines have existed for decades, and Wikipedia reports recent progress:

> Milling covers a wide variety of different operations and machines, on scales from small individual parts to large, heavy-duty gang milling operations. It is one of the most commonly used processes for machining custom parts to precise tolerances. Milling can be done with a wide range of machine tools. The original class of machine tools for milling was the milling machine (often called a mill). After the advent of computer numerical control (CNC), milling machines evolved into machining centers: milling machines augmented by automatic tool changers, tool magazines or carousels, CNC capability, coolant systems, and enclosures.[15]

Recently, a number of research projects have been initiated to look at how mobile information technologies are supporting the emergence of a *gig economy*, in which work is done outside fixed locations and set periods of time, which is certainly the case for simulated production in online virtual worlds. Well-known physical world examples are the taxi and delivery transportation companies Uber and Lyft.[16] However, even bank tellers and department store workers may find themselves working part-time now, with few if any benefits or job security, because the information systems in these businesses reduce the need for expertise and perhaps even trustworthiness on the part of the workers. Thus, the gig economy is controversial, because it may be used as a tool to reduce the power and pay of the workers. One unintended consequence may be that many part-time workers will have "free time" to devote to a future commercialized version of the maker movement, earning extra money while gaining specialized skills.

In local manufacture, as is already the case for house repair, much of the work may by its very nature be part-time, dynamic in the skills required as well as the hours invested. However, this instability may turn out to be to the benefit of energetic workers who are able to combine

---

[15] en.wikipedia.org/wiki/Milling_(machining)
[16] en.wikipedia.org/wiki/Uber; en.wikipedia.org/wiki/Lyft

two or more lines of work and are attracted to projects that are personally interesting precisely because they are not dumb, repetitive, assembly-line labor. Serious research is only just beginning, but here are excerpts of the online abstracts describing two grants from the NSF that suggest the dynamic innovation taking place in the evolving gig economy:

> **Torin Monahan**, Digital Platforms and the Mediation of Technological Change: "Digital platforms provide the fundamental infrastructure for independent contractors working in the 'gig economy' as well as for workers in the warehousing and shipping organizations that handle distribution for companies like Amazon. By generating findings about local mediation of platform capitalism, this study will produce recommendations for regional governments and firms looking to navigate these market shifts intelligently."[17]

> **Steven Sawyer**, Access to the Gig Economy: Infrastructural Competence and the Participation of Underrepresented Populations: "This research advances our understanding of how people from disadvantaged backgrounds pursue work in the so-called knowledge-based gig economy, doing contract work such as programming and writing. The research will delve into how these workers obtain, assemble, and organize digital resources, such as mobile devices, software and services, storage, security, and interconnectivity, to accomplish their jobs. These workers, especially if they lack an office, may work in coffee shops, libraries, co-working centers, and other on-the-go places. Some have routine circuits of travel and can rely on co-working spaces; some are more nomadic. Either way, they must organize and reconfigure their work resources, creating 'mobile offices' that provide cognitive space (attention), physical space (room to work), communications (relationships with others), and direct work resources. Digital technologies are usually necessary and require technical and social

---

[17] nsf.gov/awardsearch/showAward?AWD_ID=1826545

competence and financial resources. Recent studies show that this kind of work is likely to become a larger part of the future workforce."[18]

This book is not the place to outline the real-world technologies currently available for local manufacturing, or to predict their future developments, but to survey two decades of simulations that may suggest issues and innovations that could be transferred from the virtual to the real. Chapter 2 provides the necessary introduction by illustrating the experiential realism of MMO social activities, starting with observation of an online music festival in the fictional world called Middle-earth and performing a census of the 487 participants to suggest how qualitative and quantitative research can be combined. Serious research in a complex virtual world requires a phase of open-ended exploration, involving in one study of *Lord of the Rings Online* a total of 11 research avatars distributed across its 10 world-sized instances. An overview of all 30 MMOs covered in this book prepares for brief statistical analysis of data available outside two of them, a dynamic online census of millions of *World of Warcraft* avatars and a worldwide census of 27 substantial Facebook groups devoted to *Guild Wars 2* in English, Spanish, German, French, Portuguese, Polish, Hungarian, Turkish, Filipino, Thai, and Vietnamese.

Chapter 3 surveys the principles of virtual manufacturing, as a basis for understanding the social dynamics covered in later chapters. Two MMOs based in the popular Conan mythos introduce in surprising detail the evolution of human technology, from the most primitive manufacture of stone tools to the construction of physically large cities. Lacking popularity but deserving respect for their intellectual quality, *A Tale in the Desert* simulates over a period of 2 years the reconstruction of Ancient Egypt, in a context of human cooperation rather than conflict, and *Pirates of the Burning Sea* builds sailing ships in the historical context of the Caribbean in 1720. A sense of how complex simulated manufacture can become is offered by two fantasy MMOs, *Shroud of the Avatar* and *EverQuest II*.

---

[18] nsf.gov/awardsearch/showAward?AWD_ID=1665386

After these introductory chapters come two that focus on the human dynamics inside and around these virtual worlds, Chapter 4 on communication channels and Chapter 5 on social structures. Teams in the process of doing combat-oriented missions coordinate their actions in real time, able to see a good deal of information about their fellows on the computer interface, exchange durable information through text chat, and talk quickly through telephone-like systems that may be either inside or outside the MMO itself. In contrast, communications about manufacturing tend to be asynchronous and often outside the game software, prominently through text-based forums and wikis that provide product descriptions and instructions for making them, as well as taking place implicitly through leaderboards and visually in videos posted at YouTube or Twitch. Among the factors encouraging asynchronous communication is the fact that virtual production is a part-time activity that requires being at a series of specialized locations, thus not assembling all co-workers in one factory over a standard workweek, and something similar may be true for many forms of future local manufacture.

The social structures of MMOs balance dynamics with reliability, reflected in the division of labor programmed into the particular game, and through persistent player organizations that have their own communication channels and may even possess virtual headquarters and manufacturing facilities. The role and status of both a player and the player's avatar are significantly determined by the skills possessed, given that most of the time most players are not functioning within a team composed of real-world friends or family members. The skill systems give players the opportunity to make some rational decisions, notably about which skills to develop, but progress within a skill category requires considerable investment of time and effort, thus rewarding diligent workers with practical benefits and social status. Researchers have begun studying cultural variations in the organization of distributed manufacturing across nations, so research on virtual production in MMOs can by analogy be a valid way to achieve other valuable comparisons in distant virtual rather than geographic regions.[19]

---

[19] Lindtner, S., S. Bardzell, and J. Bardzell. 2016. "Reconstituting the Utopian Vision of Making: HCI After Technosolutionism." In *Proceedings of CHI'16*, 1390–402. New York, NY: ACM.

The concluding pair of chapters concerns the context in which virtual manufacture takes place. In a very real sense, the software and database of an MMO is a system combining human intelligence with artificial intelligence.[20] Much of the population is simulated by what can be called a "mob of mobs," recognizing that gamers use *mob* as a contraction for *mobiles*, identifying computer-generated beings that can move around and perform actions.[21] Their intelligence is primarily of two kinds: (1) simple *machine learning* in which events in the virtual world progressively change the numbers in some of the mob's memory registers and (2) somewhat rigid *hierarchical control systems* in which decisions made by players within a particular context determine the mob's next action. However stupid the individual mobs may be, the entire system is usually rather smart, simultaneously interacting worldwide with perhaps thousands of players. We cannot be sure which forms of artificial intelligence will be significant in the local manufacture of a particular range of products, for example, whether any of the machines will be personified like the mobs in MMOs. But clearly human workers will be interacting with complex and distributed information systems, onto which a good deal of the expertise required in the work will have been offloaded.

The concluding chapter surveys the simulated geography of virtual worlds, most of which depict really large territories, with substantially different conditions across multiple regions. One key variable is the culture of the non-player characters (NPCs), which shapes the missions that friendly ones give to players' avatars and the modes of conflict generated by unfriendly ones. Most crucially, regions differ in the skills and equipment required for successful accomplishment of missions, the rough equivalent of first-world versus third-world nations on our real planet. Long distance travel takes a long time, because it requires avatar development as well as virtual transportation, a fact that focuses attention on the immediate local region. Raw materials tend to be gathered across a limited region, whereas their use in manufacture tends to take place within a town, either in a centralized set of crafting machinery or in separate workshops. Thus,

---

[20] en.wikipedia.org/wiki/Artificial_intelligence_in_video_games
[21] Bartle, R.A. 2004. *Designing Virtual Worlds*, 102. Indianapolis, Indiana: New Riders.

MMOs do not exactly mirror the geographic realities that will shape real local manufacture, but there are significant similarities.

The past 500 years can be seen as a process of globalization of human communities, beginning with the Age of Discovery and marked today by many concerns about the possible harm caused to local communities resulting from a global economy, notably the concentration of manufacturing industries in nations with strong governments but powerless workers. Whereas computing and communication technologies have supported globalization, they also have the potential to carry us through a transition period to a time when local communities are strong again.[22] Human history does not simply follow a straight-line trajectory, but has included periods in which some form of technology and associated social structure dominated for a while before receding to only moderate influence. Most obviously, tribalism built upon small prehistoric hunter-gatherer families, expanded greatly then faded as agriculture came into economic dominance, then became nearly obsolete during the industrial age as families returned to their original small size.[23] To prepare for the best possible *postglobal future*, we need to conduct scientific research by a variety of means to develop not only the necessary technology but also appropriate forms of social organization and communication.[24]

---

[22] Freiberger, P., and M. Swaine. 1999. *Fire in the Valley: The Making of the Personal Computer*. New York, NY: McGraw-Hill; Berners-Lee, T., with Mark Fischetti. 1999. *Weaving the Web*. San Francisco: HarperSanFrancisco; Gillies, J., and R. Cailliau. 2000. *How the Web was Born*. Oxford: Oxford University Press.

[23] Childe, V.G. 1951. *Man Makes Himself*. New York, NY: New American Library; Blumberg, R.L., and R.F. Winch. 1972. "Societal Complexity and Familial Complexity: Evidence for the Curvilinear Hypothesis." *American Journal of Sociology* 77, no. 5, pp. 898–920.

[24] Bainbridge, W.S. 2019. *The Social Structure of Online Communities*. New York, NY: Cambridge University Press.

CHAPTER 2

The Universe of Online Virtual Worlds

In virtual worlds of all the kinds described in this book, people may work together to achieve goals, doing so through their computers and across Internet. In nearly all cases they are represented on their computer screens by *avatars* or *characters*, which are user-controlled virtual representations of humans. Enduring groups of players, typically called *guilds*, share private communication systems and often private virtual territory, thus simulating corporations or neighborhoods in our so-called real world. In several MMOs, guilds may set up their own crafting stations, comparable to small factories, and collectively produce virtual products of value to their avatars, such as weapons and armor, but in some cases furniture for their virtual headquarters or personal residences.

The background for considering how MMOs can be used as theoretical explorations or pilot studies for designing the local communities of the future will be presented in four parts. First, a sense of the "reality" of virtual worlds will be offered through observations and data gathered at the 2014 annual Weatherstock music festival in *Lord of the Rings Online*, which was attended by 487 people. Second, an overview of how research on the socioeconomic structures of MMOs can be done stays within the same virtual world but spans 10 different instances of it using 11 avatars as field observers. Third, a comprehensive overview of the first two decades of realistic online virtual worlds introduces the 30 MMOs explored in this research. Fourth, consideration of two high-popularity examples, *World of Warcraft* and *Guild Wars 2*, introduces the division of labor within such worlds and the extensive online communication about them that takes place in social media.

An Example of Serious Social Simulation

In selecting an example with which to begin our exploration, *Lord of the Rings Online* seemed the ideal choice, being of high quality, extreme complexity, and great cultural significance. It is based on the literary works of J.R.R. Tolkien, *The Hobbit* and *The Lord of the Rings* trilogy, that are often described as *high fantasy*.[1] Wikipedia defines this term:

> High fantasy is defined as fantasy set in an alternative, fictional ("secondary") world, rather than "the real," or "primary" world. The secondary world is usually internally consistent, but its rules differ from those of the primary world. By contrast, low fantasy is characterized by being set in the primary, or "real" world, or a rational and familiar fictional world, with the inclusion of magical elements.[2]

Although superficially accurate, I believe the label "high fantasy" is simplistic.

Tolkien was a respected academic, specializing in historical linguistics and the culture of ancient Britain.[3] He belonged to an ancient tradition, anchored in the works of Icelandic scholar Snorri Sturluson (1179–1241) whose *Prose Edda* was based on pre-Christian legends that he believed had a basis in reality, even though they had been exaggerated in retelling over the years.[4] One interpretation of Tolkien's works is that they are attempts to imagine what the *Prose Edda* of England would have been, if the legends had not been entirely forgotten, which would imply they would have connected to real preliterate history. A second interpretation is that *Lord of the Rings* is a reflection of Richard Wagner's *Ring des Nibelungen*, a set of four similarly structured German operas based on Teutonic legends,

---

[1] Tolkien, J.R.R. 1965. *The Hobbit, The Fellowship of the Ring, The Two Towers, The Return of the King.* New York, NY: Ballantine.

[2] en.wikipedia.org/wiki/The_Lord_of_the_Rings; en.wikipedia.org/wiki/High_fantasy

[3] Bainbridge, W.S. 2016. *Virtual Sociocultural Convergence*, 141–64. London: Springer.

[4] Sturluson, S. 1916. *The Prose Edda.* New York, NY: Oxford University Press.

seeking to balance the aesthetic–historic cultures between England and Germany. A third interpretation is that *Lord of the Rings* was a reaction to the horrors of the world wars of the early 20th century, by imagining four very different races of people uniting against pure evil. A fourth interpretation is that the ring in *Lord of the Rings* represents evil modern technology, comparable to but not limited to the atom bomb, and that the climax requires its destruction. This is not the place to consider the alternate interpretations in any depth, but much evidence suggests that all four are correct.

Fantasy games are not frivolous, even though some of their content is not found in exactly the same form in our real world. In high-quality fantasy and the legends of previous centuries, exotic humanoids such as Elves and Dwarves represent archetypes of human personality. In Tolkien's literary works, Orcs represent mindless brutes, thus people who do not reflect upon the meaning of life, and none of his main characters were Orcs. The Fellowship combined Elves, Dwarves, Humans, and Hobbits. Elves clearly represented scholars who loved history but tended to withdraw from mundane conflicts, but in European folklore Elves have long represented aloof kinds of people.[5] Dwarves were engineers who tried to invent technical solutions for problems. Humans were explorers but highly diverse in the behavior caused by their search for new alternatives that were neither scholarly nor technical. Hobbits apparently represented ordinary people who had minds but focused them on their immediate surroundings in their traditional provincial manner. Thus, some aspects of fantasy games are metaphoric, but metaphors can be defined as literary simulations of reality, having a somewhat abstract quality.

Lord of the Rings Online (LotRO) is a truly vast virtual world, consisting of many regions possessing different natural environments and social challenges. At the core are the home regions of the four humanoid races that collaborated in Tolkien's literature. The Hobbits live in the Shire, which contains forests, fields, streams, farms, and five towns: Hobbiton, Needlehole, Stock, Brockenborings, and Michel Delving. Each town has

---

[5] Poor, N. 2012. "Digital Elves as a Racial Other in Video Games: Acknowledgement and Avoidance." *Games and Culture* 7, no. 5, pp. 375–96.

a stable master, a nonplayer character who will rent to the player's avatar a steed that can be ridden to one of the other towns. To start with, the alternative mode of travel is walking, which can take a long time, although soon in an avatar's development it can take riding lessons and purchase a horse. The public facilities available in the towns vary, and only Michel Delving has a full set of manufacturing resources, including farmland where plants can be grown, machinery and ovens for manufacturing, plus a bank and an auction house where players may buy and sell virtual goods they have collected or produced.

West of the Shire is a region called Ered Luin where the Dwarves and Elves dwell, and east of the Shire is Bree-land, the home of Men (what Tolkien called humans) who have a very big city named Bree. As of July 2018, there were stable masters at 179 locations, most of them in other regions chiefly southeast of Bree. Like most MMO games, LotRO requires avatars to ascend a ladder of experience, which determines various characteristics of the avatar, and only the very starting location is suitable for anyone below level 5. At that point in time the top level was 115, but occasionally this level cap is increased as new and more difficult regions are added to the world. For example, the level cap was raised to 120 in October 2018, as more territory was added to the far northeast area of Middle Earth. Nearing level 20, it is safe for a new avatar to enter the region just east of Bree, Lone-lands, and reach the Forsaken Inn, the starting point for a marvelous annual festival named Weatherstock in homage to the 1969 Woodstock music and art festival that was held in our real world, with initial activities at the inn and the main music performances on a nearby mountain named Weathertop.

Weatherstock is a marvelous example of how virtual worlds can simulate real human social activities. Several players can form a long-lasting group called a *kinship* rather than the usual *guild*, and the musical bands two of my own avatars played with had set up kinships and invested in a headquarters where they could do many things, including operate their own manufacturing machinery to craft musical instruments and have a small stage where they could rehearse performances. *Lord of the Rings Online* uses the ABC notation system to control a music synthesizer, whereas an add-on program called Songbook manages communications so that an orchestra with many parts could play in a coordinated manner.[6] Using ABC, it is technically easy to compose new music as well as orchestrate traditional tunes and even quartets.[7] Online performance by musicians at different locations is generally very difficult, because the latency of the network will differ from one place to the next, but in LotRO the synthesis takes place on the computer of the individual member of the audience, so this is not a problem. The 10th annual Weatherstock was held July 21, 2018, and over the years many participants have posted music videos of these events on both Twitch and YouTube. Here are YouTube video descriptions of the two previous festivals:

Weatherstock VIII (2016)—Lord of the Rings Online: Weatherstock is LOTRO's largest annual player-run event! This music festival and competition takes place on Landroval. More information can be found at http://weatherstock.guildlaunch.com/ THANK YOU Eldalleth for your tireless efforts to stream the entirety of the event! (uploaded July 28, 2016, video duration eight hours 50 minutes)[8]

Weatherstock IX—2017 Full Broadcast: Here is the full archive of this year's livestreamed broadcast of Weatherstock on Twitch. tv/LOTROstream. Thanks to Eldalleth, StinePlays, Druidsfire, and everyone else who volunteered to help out on Twitch, and all of the bands and organizers in-game who put this massive event together. Also, thanks to everyone who stopped by either in-game or on Twitch! (uploaded July 24, 2017, video duration: eight hours 59 minutes)[9]

[6] Bainbridge, W.S. 2014. *An Information Technology Surrogate for Religion: The Veneration of Deceased Family Members in Online Games*, 120–33. New York, NY: Palgrave Macmillan.

[7] en.wikipedia.org/wiki/ABC_notation

[8] www.youtube.com/watch?v=i7KYNZIeLWQ&t=83s

[9] www.youtube.com/watch?v=u3qWl53NOD4

The phrase "takes place on Landroval" refers to the fact that 10 different versions of LotRO existed, operating in parallel but off separate Internet server systems, and Landroval is the name of one of them. Five of the 10 "worlds" serve North America. The other five serve Europe, two in English, two in German, and one in French, although users can individually decide which of these languages their interface text should be in. In November 2018 two more servers were added, called "legendary" because they were limited to the territories included when LotRO launched in 2007, and to experience levels 1 to 50, with plans to add the other areas and levels in the same sequence that had been followed over the subsequent decade.

I created an avatar specifically to attend the 2014 Weatherstock, naming him Ogburn in honor of the technological determinist sociologist William F. Ogburn. In LotRO and many other popular MMOs, each avatar must be permanently assigned to a *class* of adventurers, so he was a minstrel that would harmonize with a music festival. Optionally, avatars may learn professional skills, and in LotRO they are clustered in trios called *vocations*. Ogburn became a woodsman, which combined these more specialized professions: woodworker, forester, farmer. A woodworker could make musical instruments, and a forester could gather the necessary wood from the forests. The farmer profession was incidental, and another vocation called armsman had woodworker as its incidental profession, because an armsman cannot gather wood but must obtain it from other avatars who possess the forester profession.

Table 2.1 shows statistics on the participants at Weatherstock 2014, based on the 334 avatars who participated in the informal part of the festival, playing or listening to music just outside the Forsaken Inn, and the 487 who attended the main part up on Weathertop. For online virtual gatherings in 2014, these numbers are remarkably high. Each avatar represented a person and wore distinctive clothing. The graphic display did tend to lag as people moved around, and only at smaller music events are members of the audience encouraged to dance. But the synthesized music itself was not affected. The table shows the distribution of avatar classes, offering a brief standard description of each and arranging them in descending order of popularity among the 487, who include the vast majority of the 334. This census was taken with a portion of

Table 2.1 Census of avatars by class in Weatherstock 2014

Class	Forsaken	Weathertop	Description of class
Minstrel	32.6%	34.7%	Heart of a fellowship, herald of hope, inspiration, renewal
Hunter	20.7%	20.1%	Master of field and forest
Burglar	8.4%	7.4%	Master of stealth and misdirection
Champion	6.0%	7.4%	Consummate warrior, unrelenting in battle
Guardian	7.5%	7.0%	Protector of the weak and defender of those in need
Lore-master	8.1%	7.0%	Seeker of knowledge and a guardian of wisdom
Warden	4.8%	6.2%	Mobile melee combatant
Captain	6.6%	5.3%	Masterful leader, commanding presence, strengthens allies
Rune-keeper	5.4%	4.9%	Mystical linguist and master of true names
Total	100.0%	100.0%	
	334	487	

the user interface that lets players see who is currently online, especially in the vicinity, in order to team up for missions that individuals cannot accomplish solo.

Not surprisingly, minstrels were the most common class in attendance, although any of the classes could play a musical instrument if they received training from a minstrel. Given J.R.R. Tolkien's opposition to magic, LotRO's designers were forced to find ways of offering players magical abilities, but interpreting them in nonmagical terms. A minstrel plays music during battle, with various kinds of tune affecting the outcome just as varied magical spells might do. Having run a lore-master up to the maximum experience level of 115, I have seen how that complex class exercises naturalistic magic, and the same is true for rune-keepers. For example, a lore-master can acquire and train animal companions, and mine primarily used a bear who became very strong and eventually did nearly all the fighting, having become nearly invincible over hundreds of hours of action.

One might guess that hunters are numerous in the Weatherstock 2014 census because they are good solo characters, and many players with their main avatars on other servers might have created a hunter on Landroval specifically to attend Weatherstock, which does require getting at least a short distance up the experience ladder without help from a kinship. However, several censuses I have carried out across all the servers found that in general about 20 percent of the avatars are hunters, while minstrels tend to constitute about 12 percent, suggesting how collection of statistical data in virtual worlds can be used to test as well as to frame hypotheses. The overwhelming majority of the 487 avatars present at the peak of the festival were audience rather than performers. It is common for players to have multiple characters, although one would need multiple accounts and computers to operate more than one at any given time, what is called *multiboxing* and not common in role-playing games.

The example of Weatherstock uses the primary research methodologies employed in this book. One cannot study a culturally complex cultural world without performing extensive observational research, what cultural anthropologists call *ethnography* and what sociologists call *participant observation*. But comprehensive study must go beyond the energetic development of personal experience, in three ways. First, as Table 2.1 illustrates, data about large social groups and populations must also be collected, often in quantitative form. Second, connections must be made to immediately relevant information outside the virtual world, such as reading Tolkien's books and viewing YouTube videos. Third, whether done by an individual researcher or a community of researchers, any virtual world must be compared with others, ideally developing some form of classification scheme as well as comparing details of their technical features.

Open-Ended Exploration of Middle-Earth

Although the goals of this book primarily concern drawing abstract lessons that might apply to specific real-world systems that the games only simulated, the precondition is direct experience. For purposes of reasonably comprehensive research, I created 11 characters, tried all races, classes, and vocations, as well as collected quantitative data on all 10 servers of *Lord of the Rings Online*. Table 2.2 lists these virtual research assistants, thereby providing a more comprehensive perspective on the diversity of avatars and the choices open to players. The research was done in several phases, beginning August 9, 2009, and ending July 4, 2018. While operating an avatar, one can enter into the text chat "/played" and get information on the total time that particular avatar was played. The total for the 11 was 1,351 hours. With the exception of *World of Warcraft* which I explored for over 3,000 hours, most other examples referred to in this book took less time, the 1,187 hours in *Star Wars: The Old Republic* and 618 hours in *Star Wars Galaxies* being among the highest. Dedicated players invest similar fractions of their lives in these virtual worlds.

The 11 avatars vary significantly in the number of hours each was played and the experience level they achieved up a status ladder from 1 to 115, a reflection in part of the different roles they played in a series of research projects. Recently, LotRO added to the four Tolkien "races" the High Elf variant of Elves and the Beorning variant of Man, the latter of which could temporarily take the form of fierce bears. The lore-master class and historian vocation were selected for the main avatar, Rumilisoun, as her chief task was documentation of the cultures of Middle-earth, and a leading computer science publication printed her avatarish personal views on that important topic.[10]

Originally, there were two research avatars, Rumilisoun and Angusmcintosh, who were both on the Gladden world, a North American server, tasked with performing general ethnography of the fictional culture. The two avatars named Andraeda were added later, to serve as assistants to Angusmcintosh in a linguistics study on two European servers, Laurelin which used the English language and Belagaer which used the German. Angusmcintosh was named after the real-world student of J.R.R. Tolkien who established what is now known as the Angus McIntosh Centre for Historical Linguistics at the University of Edinburgh.[11] Ogburn was added to study the musicology of LotRO, and the English-language variant of Andraeda also performed this function. In order to collect more

---

[10] Rumilisoun. 2010. "Rebirth of Worlds." *Communications of the ACM* 53, no. 12, p. 128.

[11] www.amc.lel.ed.ac.uk

Table 2.2 Eleven research avatars in one virtual world

Name	World	Hours	Level	Gender	Race	Class	Vocation
Rumilisoun	Gladden	791	115	Female	Elf	Lore-master	Historian
Ogburn	Landroval	174	108	Male	Dwarf	Minstrel	Woodsman
Andraeda	Laurelin	88	25	Female	Man	Minstrel	Tinker
Angusmcintosh	Crickhollow	63	25	Male	Hobbit	Burglar	Historian
Aeleven	Brandywine	60	35	Male	Elf	Hunter	Armourer
Andraeda	Belagaer	42	25	Female	Man	Minstrel	Yeoman
Fitchperkins	Arkenstone	41	25	Female	Man	Captain	Tinker
Catullus	Gwaihir	37	25	Male	High Elf	Rune-keeper	Armsman
Meglivorn	Sirannon	21	25	Male	Beorning	Beorning	Explorer
Gimloing	Landroval	20	5	Male	Dwarf	Champion	Tinker
Bolivianita	Evernight	14	50	Female	Hobbit	Hunter	Explorer

extensive data for the present project, Angusmcintosh was moved from the Gladden server to the Crickhollow server, for a modest transfer payment, and the other avatars were created.

The Gimloing avatar was added near the end of this research, for a specific experiment on manufacturing, in which Gimloing would stay all the time at a manufacturing facility, and Ogburn would collect raw materials and ship them to Gimloing, thereby illustrating the smallest possible economy. Gimloing was given the tinker vocation, which is the only one that includes the jeweler profession. Ogburn then switched from woodsman to explorer vocation, which preserved his forester skills but required him to learn prospecting (gathering metal and gemstones) and tailoring. For clarity, here are the professions in their vocations: tinker (jeweler, prospector, cook), explorer (tailor, forester, prospector).

A prospector can gain general experience from gathering raw materials but not professional skill which requires processing them, notably going to a public forge like one on the west side of Bree and melting metal into ingots. This meant that Ogburn needed to do not only enough prospecting to level both of them up in this skill, but also collect the raw materials needed for Gimloing's jeweler profession. Ogburn could level up his forester skill by killing animals and processing their hides, and level his tailor profession by making things from those hides. Neither could acquire the raw materials needed for Gimloing's cook profession, so they were bought from the player auction house with money primarily gathered by Ogburn, but also earned when Gimloing sold his products in the auction house or to nonplayer vendors. The 20 hours invested in Gimloing allowed him to complete learning the most advanced of 11 levels of all of his professional skills, but Ogburn's labor investment accomplishing the same goal was rather greater.

A key purpose of the Ogburn–Gimloing partnership was to highlight the geographically fixed nature of manufacture, in contrast to the roaming nature of resource collection. To collect all the resources needed to make the highest-rated products in the prospecting and jeweler professions, Ogburn needed to travel all over Middle-earth, which required him to have reached the adventuring experience level of 105, exactly 100 steps higher up the status ladder than Gimloing was allowed to achieve. The only traveling required of Gimloing was walking back and forth, between three rooms of Thorin's Hall, the main castle of the Dwarves. One held the forges that could melt ore into metal ingots, which advanced the prospector profession. Another provided an oven for cooking and a workbench for jewelry. The third room offered access to the auction system through which Gimloing could purchase the raw ingredients for cooking sold by other players who did farming. Ogburn and Gimloing never met, because Ogburn had two ways to ship the raw materials he collected to Gimloing. If he happened to be in a town that had a bank, they shared a bank account where he could deposit items that Gimloing could withdraw from a banker in Thorin's Hall. But at a much larger number of locations, Ogburn could at low cost mail materials to Gimloing. Note the rather complex division of functions in this example—resource gathering, transportation, and manufacture—which only hint at the full complexity of *Lord of the Rings Online*.

This somewhat ornate and limited experiment highlights more general principles. First, in LotRO, but not in many other gameworlds, performing professions earns general experience, although it does so efficiently only at low levels of experience. Yet the table reports that Gimloing never got above experience level 5. One other avatar, Andraeda of Belagaer, earned half of her 25 levels of general experience by practicing the yeoman vocation which combines these professions: farmer, cook, tailor. Farming a field on the outskirts of Michel Delving, she grew many of the ingredients for cooking, which she performed at a nearby public oven. Gimloing could have achieved level 25 of experience, rather than just 5, by doing his manufacturing, so why did he not?

In LotRO, it is possible to buy experience, or to buy a relic that can halt gains in experience. In an online store accessed within the game, one may buy a special currency called LotRO Points, in various deals, from 600 points for $7.99 (75 per dollar) to 23,000 points for $199.99 (115 per dollar). For 100 points, a relic called Stone of the Tortoise was purchased and placed in Gimloing's pocket, halting his experience progress so long as it was there. Ogburn's case was practically the opposite. He reached level 48 by the usual arduous effort, but then jumped to 105 by using Aria of the Valar, which cost 6,695 points. He wandered for a while, getting used to his exaggerated status, ascending just to level 106, and then collaborating with Gimloing took him only to level 108. Bolivianita leapt from level 6 to level 50, using Gift of the Valar, which cost 3,995 points, and most of her mere 14 hours of work were invested simply in collecting quantitative data for a vocation-related study that required data from all 10 worlds. All the other avatars earned their status "honestly."

This example connects to two questions regarding online games, neither of which has been answered definitely: First, how can the companies that produce the game earn decent profits? Second, what forms of sociotechnological system fairly reward people for their skills and efforts?[12] Ordinary solo-player games, over the years, have been sold outright to each customer, which seems straightforward enough, although one continuing issue concerns what might prevent the owner of a game from loaning it to friends, as one can do with a printed novel. The classic "cost recovery" method, exemplified by *World of Warcraft* and many of its competitors around the time of its launch in 2004, was to sell the game, but require a monthly subscription to access it online after a brief initial period.

Once the highly competitive market for online games was well developed, many games became *free to play*, earning profits by selling virtual items through the game, using virtual currencies like LotRO points. In the worst cases, games became *pay to win*, allowing rich players called *whales* to buy armor, weapons, vehicles, and other power-enhancing virtual goods. This complex economic situation cannot be fully explored here, but does sometimes affect player manufacture of virtual goods, because they may become stuck in an implicit competition with the game company. LotRO and other culturally sophisticated games face a quandary, needing to make money but wanting to avoid competing against players, so they tend to sell luxury goods, such as more beautiful clothing, or items that do not duplicate the ones players can create.

Two Decades of Virtual Gameworlds

At the risk of oversimplification, we might say that several sports, such as baseball and football, consolidated in the 19th century. The history of

---

[12] Castronova, E. 2005. *Synthetic Worlds: The Business and Culture of Online Games*. Chicago: University of Chicago Press.

computer games is complex, but unless one goes wild with metaphors, this field emerged in the second half of the 20th century and is still undergoing unpredictable development today. I owned my first computer game in 1956, and it was a Geniac, designed as a computer science educational tool by Edmund C. Berkeley, cofounder of the Association for Computing Machinery.[13] Setting aside electric pinball games and their turn-taking ilk, arguably the first multiplayer computer game was *Spacewar!* dating from 1962.[14] The earliest online example studied for this project was the fantasy game *Ultima Online* dating from 1997.

Whatever exact terminology we wish to apply to *Lord of the Rings Online* and *Ultima Online*, both are considered fantasy games, the genre that dominated the field for most of its first two decades. LotRO launched in 2007, coincidentally one decade after UO, and even in 2004 *World of Warcraft* was able to offer much better graphics than UO, which used oblique projection that viewed the world from a set point overhead and lacked perspective, whereas the WoW viewpoint could be adjusted and displayed objects on the horizon as small as they would appear in the real world. Both share with LotRO the goals of depicting adventures in an imaginary world that has some similarity with the European Middle Ages, yet adds some explicitly magical features. The oldest science fiction game considered here is *Anarchy Online* which dates from 2001, the same year the historical *World War II Online* launched. Table 2.3 lists the 30 virtual worlds that were studied for this project.

Table 2.3 **A universe of 30 online virtual worlds**

MMO name	Launch year	Wikipedia views	Wiki articles	Subreddit subscribers	MMORPG category
Ultima Online	1997	378,841	2,992	3,548	Fantasy
EverQuest	1999	617,621	1,509	7,780	Fantasy
Anarchy Online	2001	104,433	800	1,394	Sci-Fi
Dark Age of Camelot	2001	179,424	1,860	1,635	Fantasy

---

[13] en.wikipedia.org/wiki/Geniac

[14] en.wikipedia.org/wiki/Spacewar!

RuneScape	2001	1,182,555	43,949	136,390	Fantasy
World War II Online	2001	102,038	Many	310	Historical
A Tale in the Desert	2003	22,420	Many	112	Historical
Entropia Universe	2003	366,379	1,624	612	Sci-Fi
EVE Online	2003	1,002,775	1,880	101,089	Sci-Fi
Star Wars Galaxies	2003	444,972	9,680	3,087	Sci-Fi
City of Heroes	2004	497,123	5,645	2,850	Super-Hero
EverQuest II	2004	169,396	181,533	2,601	Fantasy
World of Warcraft	2004	3,776,547	182,467	839,010	Fantasy
Guild Wars	2005	269,497	21,728	12,615	Fantasy
Lord of the Rings Online	2007	318,376	84,201	16,408	Fantasy
Tabula Rasa	2007	135,025	2,825	None	Sci-Fi
Age of Conan	2008	144,018	7,091	356	Fantasy
Pirates of the Burning Sea	2008	66,515	5,904	80	Historical
Fallen Earth	2009	40,866	22,252	220	Sci-Fi
Star Trek Online	2010	502,617	14,779	19,650	Sci-Fi
Gods and Heroes	2011	19,302	64	12	Historical
Star Wars: The Old Republic	2011	2,098,397	33,338	79,648	Sci-Fi
Xsyon: Prelude	2011	7,959	64	29	Sci-Fi
Guild Wars 2	2012	694,776	79,983	188,599	Fantasy
Defiance	2013	239,054	341	5,174	Sci-Fi
Wildstar	2014	271,742	5,627	26,990	Sci-Fi
Elder Scrolls Online	2015	1,744,247	61,313	164,462	Fantasy
Black Desert Online	2016	738,030	861	85,410	Fantasy
Conan Exiles	2018	395,633	4,278	27,441	Fantasy
Shroud of the Avatar	2018	191,625	8,842	336	Fantasy

All 30 MMOs have Wikipedia articles, and the most popular have many secondary pages linked from the main page, such as a page for each expansion of the virtual territory over the years. From the "view history" tab of a Wikipedia page, one may access statistics, like the number of times the page was viewed in the period from July 1, 2015 until "today" which was October 7, 2018, for the Wikipedia views column of Table 2.3. All 30 cases have their own wikis, in some cases more than one, often at the fansite Wikia.com, and the wiki articles column lists the number of articles on the biggest wiki, acknowledging that the wikis use very different criteria to report their size, which two chose not to do at all. It is difficult to compare the popularity of MMOs, because they do not report their number of players, but a website called mmo-population. com suggests that a proxy measure would be the number of subscribers to the game's subreddit on the forum site reddit.com. A very active online blogsite, MMORPG.com, discusses all of these 30 extensively and classifies most of them as fantasy, sci-fi, and historical.[15] As of the date for these data, four of the MMOs had shut down: *Tabula Rasa* (in 2009), *Star Wars Galaxies* (2011), *City of Heroes* (2012), and *Gods and Heroes* (2012). Two others were scheduled to be shut down before the end of 2018: *Pirates of the Burning Sea* and *Wildstar*.

There are many serious approaches to the analysis of these human–technical systems, and one obvious example is *game theory*, proposed in *Theory of Games and Economic Behavior* by John von Neumann and Oskar Morgenstern back in 1944.[16] An alternative school of thought, largely founded by Johan Huizinga and Donald Winnicott, considers play to be an essential component of culture and of individual psychological development.[17] In sociology, a vast diversity of literature exists concerning role-playing, and these games are all social role-playing systems.[18] Yet the

[15] www.mmorpg.com/games-list

[16] von Neumann, J., and O. Morgenstern. 1944. *Theory of Games and Economic Behavior*. Princeton, New Jersey: Princeton University Press.

[17] Huizinga, J. 1938. *Homo Ludens: A Study of the Play-Element in Culture*. London: Routledge and Paul, K. 1971. *Donald Woods Winnicott, Playing and Reality*. London: Tavistock.

[18] Mead, G.H. 1934. *Mind, Self, and Society*. Chicago: University of Chicago Press; Goffman, E. 1959. *The Presentation of Self in Everyday Life*. Garden City, New York, NY: Doubleday.

most important theorists in this field are not academics, but the design-ers of the games themselves, who function within a highly sophisticated culture, having its own perspectives on human behavior, as well as con-siderable technical expertise.[19] Therefore, this book will primarily follow the strictures of *grounded theory*, seeking to extract insights from the cases under study, rather than imposing a pre-existing theoretical structure on the data.[20]

The classic example is a game—and indeed an entire genre of games—called *Kriegspiel*, which is German for *war game*. As Wikipedia reports, it

> was a system used for training officers in the Prussian and German armies. The first set of rules was created in 1812 and named *Instructions for the Representation of Tactical Maneuvers under the Guise of a Wargame*. It was originally produced and developed further by Lieutenant Georg Leopold von Reiswitz and his son Georg Heinrich Rudolf von Reiswitz of the Prussian Army.[21]

A 2009 article in the German news magazine *Der Spiegel* noted: "Die Regeln, nach denen Reiswitz' Spielleiter den Spielverlauf zu berechnen hatte, sind konstruiert, um in der Spielwelt eine Realität so glaubwürdig wie möglich zu simulieren. Reiswitz' Vorgehen dabei erinnert an heu-tige Rollenspiele."[22] Google Translate renders this into English as: "The rules by which Reiswitz's game master had to calculate the gameplay are designed to simulate a reality in the game world as believably as possi-ble. Reiswitz's approach is reminiscent of today's role-playing games." The technical term *Spielleiter* is correctly translated as *game master*, equivalent to a game designer who sets up the initial conditions and may also judge the performance of the players.

---

[19] Paul, C.A. 2011. "Optimizing Play: How Theorycraft Changes Gameplay and Design." *Game Studies* 11, no. 2, pp. 1–14.

[20] Glaser, B.G., and A.L. Strauss. 1967. *The Discovery of Grounded Theory: Strate-gies for Qualitative Research*. Chicago: Aldine.

[21] en.wikipedia.org/wiki/Kriegsspiel_(wargame)

[22] Lischka, K. 2009. "Wie PreußischeMilitärs den Rollenspiel-AhnenErfanden." *Spiegel Online*, www.spiegel.de/netzwelt/spielzeug/kriegsspiel-wie-preussische-militaers-den-rollenspiel-ahnen-erfanden-a-625745.html

Role-playing games, and games involving economic properties, were common throughout the 20th century. Especially noteworthy was the predecessor of the popular board game, *Monopoly*, called *The Landlord Game* and patented in 1904 by Elizabeth Magie, who created it as an educational tool:

> She based the game on the economic principles of Georgism, a system proposed by Henry George, with the object of demonstrating how rents enrich property owners and impoverish tenants. She knew that some people could find it hard to understand why this happened and what might be done about it, and she thought that if Georgist ideas were put into the concrete form of a game, they might be easier to demonstrate.[23]

Less didactic and more role-oriented were two sleuth and psychological mid-century board games, *Mr. Ree!* and *Clue* or *Cluedo*. *Mr. Ree!* dates from 1937 and a gamesite describes its dynamic nature:

> Each player assumes the part of one of the Characters in Aunt Cora's red brick house, and by his actions and positions in the house-hold follows thru with his likes and dislikes of the various persons with whom fate has placed him. The player, represented on the board by a hollow token, roams about inside and outside the house, choosing and concealing weapons with which to commit a crime. The strong arm of the law, in the person of Mr. Ree, is ever present patrolling the grounds surrounding the house.[24]

The 1949 board game *Clue* requires players

to determine who murdered the game's victim… where the crime took place, and which weapon was used. Each player assumes the role of one of the six suspects, and attempts to deduce the correct

---

[23]   en.wikipedia.org/wiki/The_Landlord%27s_Game; en.wikipedia.org/wiki/Monopoly_(game)

[24]   boardgamegeek.com/boardgame/2924/mr-ree-fireside-detective

answer by strategically moving around a game board representing the rooms of a mansion and collecting clues about the circumstances of the murder from the other players.[25]

A revolutionary development was the emergence of *Dungeons and Dragons* (D&D) in 1974, a tabletop role-playing game that allowed players to invent their own stories or follow an increasing number of partially prewritten scripts, usually within a fantasy environment that was frankly influenced by *Lord of the Rings*, but avoided copyright infringement by calling Hobbits *halflings* instead.[26] Another one of the many influences was *jetan*, a chesslike game devised by Edgar Rice Burroughs for *Chessmen of Mars*, one of a series of novels that also influenced the *Star Wars* mythos and that embedded the gameplay in the fictional history of competing alien ethnicities.[27] Wikipedia summarizes this complex cultural system:

> D&D departs from traditional wargaming and assigns each player a specific character to play instead of a military formation. These characters embark upon imaginary adventures within a fantasy setting. A Dungeon Master serves as the game's referee and storyteller while maintaining the setting in which the adventures occur, and playing the role of the inhabitants. The characters form a party that interacts with the setting's inhabitants, and each other. Together they solve dilemmas, engage in battles, and gather treasure and knowledge. In the process the characters earn experience points in order to rise in levels, and become increasingly powerful over a series of sessions.[28]

A variant of D&D, *Neverwinter Nights*, is said to have been "the first multiplayer online role-playing game to display graphics, and ran from 1991 to 1997 on AOL."[29]

---

[25] en.wikipedia.org/wiki/Cluedo

[26] Gygax, G. 1979. *Advanced Dungeons and Dragons, Dungeon Masters Guide*. New York, NY: TSR/Random House.

[27] Burroughs, E.R. 1922. *Chessmen of Mars*. Chicago: A.C. McClurg.

[28] en.wikipedia.org/wiki/Dungeons_%26_Dragons

[29] en.wikipedia.org/wiki/Neverwinter_Nights_(1991_video_game)

The most influential MMO of these decades was *World of Warcraft* (WoW), which clearly was influenced by D&D, but that was the fourth in a series of games. In 1994, *Warcraft: Orcs and Humans* launched, a real-time strategy computer game, not a role-playing game, in which two players controlled competing armies as in chess, or one person played against the computer. It connected to *Lord of the Rings* through the fact that one of the two opposing factions was Orcs, and it had some of the same overarching narrative structure as jetan. *Warcraft II* was released in 1996, and *Warcraft III* in 2002, both also being two-player strategy games that expanded upon the narrative in an increasingly complete technical context. In 2004, *World of Warcraft* employed the same mythos and expanded it further, in the massively multiplayer role-playing genre. At that point in the history of the genre, *EverQuest* dating from 1999 was already well established, with a fantasy mythos not very different from WoW, and *EverQuest II* was launching almost simultaneously. WoW quickly became the most popular MMO and was widely perceived to be more pleasant, more coherent, and less difficult than the *EverQuest* games.

Game designers are also game players, and individuals often move from one company to another. Reportedly, the team that created *Guild Wars* included veterans from the *Warcraft* series. The original *Guild Wars* was a series of three separately purchased but connected games that did not require a monthly subscription fee. *Guild Wars II* is quite different, offering a more integrated virtual world, and like WoW was based on its own mythos that was similar to *Lord of the Rings* but not derived from any specific earlier stories.[30] Because of these similarities and differences, these are good examples with which to conclude this chapter.

Two Vast Worlds

Given its great popularity, *World of Warcraft* has been the focus of considerable scholarly research.[31] It draws part of its mythos from *Lord of the*

[30] Lummis, M., P. Kathleen, K. Edwin, and R. Kurt. 2012. *Guild Wars 2*. Indianapolis, Indiana: BradyGames.
[31] Bainbridge, W.S. 2010. *The Warcraft Civilization: Social Science in a Virtual World*. Cambridge, Massachusetts: MIT Press.

Rings, for example, allowing avatars to be Dwarves or Elves, and even Orcs. Many sources of statistical data are available, including an official online database called Battle.Net where the roster of current members of the Science guild I founded a decade ago can be seen.[32] Of the 173 current members, here are the numbers for the available races in this particular guild as of August 30, 2018: 55 Blood Elves, 19 Goblins, 10 Orcs, 13 Pandarens, 34 Taurens, 20 Trolls, and 22 Undeads. Clearly this is a fantasy world, but it has connections to three real-world cultures: Chinese (Pandarens), Native Americans of western North America (Taurens), and Afro-Caribbeans (Trolls). We see no characters in this guild who are called Humans, because it belongs to the Horde, one of two competing factions, and Humans dominate the other faction, the Alliance. Realm Pop, an extensive but unofficial online WoW dataset, offered data on fully 80,502,616 characters on December 12, 2017.[33] Table 2.4 illustrates how it is possible to analyze such data in meaningful ways, with census information about two kinds of Elves in *World of Warcraft*.

In the WoW mythos, centuries ago an advanced culture of High Elves had flourished, rather similar to the Elves in Tolkien's mythos. But they played with advanced technology, causing a geological catastrophe and disintegration of their civilization. Today, they are split into two opposing cultures. The Night Elves are environmentalists who formed the Alliance with Humans, worshipping the moon goddess Elune and devoted to the preservation of Nature.[34] The Blood Elves have responded in the opposite way to the ancient catastrophe, becoming intense secularists who seek to gain absolute power over technology and thus over Nature. The most popular of 14 races was Humans with 16.8 percent, but Blood Elves were a close second at 15.4 percent, and Night Elves were in third place with 11.7 percent. Table 2.4 lists the 11 classes of characters, for example, priests whose main job is healing allies during battle, and warriors who engage in hand-to-hand melee fighting, among the Elves. Note that nearly a third of Night Elves are druids, a quasi-religious group devoted

---

[32] us.battle.net/wow/en/guild/earthen-ring/Science/roster?sort=lvl&dir=a

[33] realmpop.com

[34] Nardi, B. 2010. *My Life as a Night Elf Priest: An Anthropological Account of World of Warcraft*. Ann Arbor, Michigan: University of Michigan Press.

Table 2.4 An Elven census in World of Warcraft

Class of avatar	Race		Gender		Region	
	Night Elf	Blood Elf	Male	Female	America	Europe
Death knight	7.4%	11.3%	11.1%	8.4%	9.8%	9.4%
Demon hunter	15.8%	12.6%	16.3%	11.9%	13.4%	14.5%
Druid	33.1%	0.0%	13.5%	14.9%	13.6%	15.1%
Hunter	15.6%	9.9%	11.6%	13.0%	12.7%	12.0%
Mage	4.1%	10.5%	6.8%	8.5%	7.9%	7.5%
Monk	3.1%	4.7%	3.5%	4.5%	4.1%	3.9%
Paladin	0.0%	20.7%	13.7%	10.1%	11.7%	11.8%
Priest	6.4%	10.4%	5.8%	11.1%	8.6%	8.7%
Rogue	8.8%	7.7%	7.9%	8.4%	8.3%	8.0%
Warlock	0.0%	7.7%	3.8%	4.8%	4.7%	4.0%
Warrior	5.8%	4.6%	6.0%	4.3%	5.1%	5.1%
Total	100.0%	100.0%	100.0%	100.0%	100.0%	100.0%
Cases	9,428,227	12,396,407	9,986,374	11,838,260	11,591,818	10,232,816

to Nature, whereas absolutely none of the Blood Elves belong to this class, simply because the game software prohibits this sacrilege. In contrast, Night Elves are not allowed to become paladins, who are warrior priests, or warlocks.

The gender columns in the table refer to the gender of the characters, not that of their players. Across all races tallied in the dataset, the percent of avatars that were female was 39.4. The percent female of avatars varied significantly across the Tolkien races in the Realm Pop data: 42.4 percent among Humans, 56.5 percent among Blood Elves, 56.3 percent among Night Elves, only 14.5 percent among Dwarves, and 21.1 percent among Orcs. Note that the percent of healing priests is higher among female characters, 11.1 percent versus 5.8 percent for males, whereas males are overrepresented in the more violent classes: death knight, demon hunter, paladin, and warrior. The two concluding columns of the table compare characters whose players are in North America with those in Europe, showing very small differences but illustrating how external variables can sometimes be brought into this kind of analysis.

Nonviolent gathering and crafting skills are significant in *World of Warcraft*, although not quite matching their prominence in *Lord of the Rings Online*. *Guild Wars 2* has a comparably complex manufacturing system in which crafting contributes significantly to advancement in general experience, as does peaceful exploration of the world's geography. In *Guild Wars 2*, I was able to take four characters to that game's experience cap of 80 and explore rather thoroughly in 384 hours, one of the characters completely avoiding any of the violent adventures and primarily advancing by doing crafting with natural resources and money gathered by one of the other characters. A website similar to Realm Pop, but called GW2Armory, reports that fully 54 percent of the registered characters are female, demographic evidence that GW2's style is different from that of WoW, even though they have many structural and technical similarities.[35]

Whereas much of the focus of this book will be inside the virtual worlds, it is important to realize that they have external dimensions as well, what I have called the *penumbra*, a shadow cast by a virtual world on the real world. For example, Table 2.5 lists the 27 *Guild Wars 2* groups

[35] gw2armory.com/statistics

Table 2.5 Large social media groups oriented toward Guild Wars 2

Facebook ID	Name	Type	Members	Language
GuildWars2andXPs	Guild Wars 2 and Expansions	Closed	18,407	English
GW2Gamers	Guild Wars 2	Closed	15,541	English
news.guildwars2	Guild Wars 2 Germany	Closed	9,696	German
179753682096794	Guild Wars 2—Brasil	Closed	7,275	Portuguese
GW2Latino	Guild Wars 2 Latino [NA]	Closed	6,599	Spanish
393356807431335	Thai Guild Wars2	Closed	5,075	Thai
guildwars2girls	Guild Wars 2 Girls	Closed	5,062	English
124335194248044	Guild Wars 2! Il gruppoitaliano!	Closed	4,872	Italian
464931967031760	Guild wars 2 Comunidad Latina Original	Closed	3,717	Spanish
GW2Casuals	Guild Wars 2 Casuals	Closed	3,004	English
guildwars2philippines	Guild Wars 2 Philippines—Buy and Sell	Closed	2,710	English+
guildwars2polska	Guild Wars 2 Polska	Closed	2,588	Polish
1529725287286963	Guild Wars 2—France	Closed	2,078	French
GuildWars2Thailand	Guild Wars 2 Thailand	Closed	1,600	Thai
124439867574775	Guild Wars 2 Hungary	Public	1,597	Hungarian
GuildWars2PvP	Guild Wars 2 PvP	Closed	1,568	English
gw2ph	Guild Wars 2 Philippines	Public	1,543	Filipino
gw2mex	Guild Wars 2 México [MEX]	Closed	1,467	Spanish
openguildwarsbrasil	Guild Wars 2 Brasil	Public	1,195	Portuguese
vietnamesevodka	Guild Wars 2—Vietnamese Vodka	Closed	1,114	Vietnamese
gw2comprayventa	Guild Wars 2 Compra y venta	Closed	1,050	Spanish
spvpbrasil	[sPvP] Comunidadebrasileira Guild Wars 2	Closed	1,039	Portuguese
sanctumofrall	Guild Wars 2: Sanctum of Rall	Public	956	English
guildwars2turkiye	Guild Wars 2 Türkiye	Closed	898	Turkish

Baruchbay	Guild Wars 2 Bahía de Baruch	Closed	662	Spanish
guildwars2ph	Guild Wars 2 PH	Closed	530	Unknown
220297651315407	Guild Wars 2 [Malta]	Public	514	English

found in Facebook on August 25, 2018, that had at least 500 members. Real-world crafting of the future may often be organized in cooperative guilds—as was true centuries ago and today in virtual worlds—and also communicate semiformally through tomorrow's social media. As their names suggest, two of the groups emphasize PvP play, in which *player-versus-player* combat is emphasized, but *Guild Wars 2* primarily emphasizes the more cooperative PvE, or player-versus-environment, kind of activity in which enemies are non-player characters.

As an example of how people worldwide help each other, following are excerpts from a discussion that took place early August 2018 in the biggest group, Guild Wars 2 and Expansions. A player in Myanmar sought advice on how to increase an unspecified crafting skill, using the standard abbreviation "lvl" for "level." Although crafting builds regular experience on a scale of 1 to 80 levels, abbreviated in the following as "exp," the normal levels for each production craft go from 1 to 400, after which progress roughly doubles in difficulty up to the cap at level 500, at which the avatar earns "grandmaster" status.[36] The terms "legendary" and "ascended" refer to the highest quality items.[37] Other terms will be explained as follows:

> Player in Myanmar: Whats the fastest way to lvl up crafting? My lvl is too low to craft some materials.
> Player in California: I use gw2crafts.net
> Player in Australia: I use it as well. Make sure you use your api key so you don't buy excess if you dont need to.
> Player in Greece: Gw2crafts you will need to spend some gold however.

---

[36] wiki.guildwars2.com/wiki/Crafting#Skill_level
[37] wiki.guildwars2.com/wiki/Item#Quality

Player in Indonesia: Calm down and level your character first. Crafting does not really come into play unless you craft legendary or ascended. Gather and deposit materials as you level up your character as future investments or sell them for quick money.

Player in Romania: To lvl craft while you lvl character.

Player in Myanmar: I'm already lvl 80 but I didn't lvl up crafting.

Player in Romania: hahaha delete character and start again.

Player in Canada: Your guild hall should have a buff for crafting bonus and use a booster that gives craft exp bonus and then just craft.

Player in England: Discover new recipes.

Player in unknown location: I found it best to do it all in one sitting if you can. Get the guild buff and any booster buffs and then level it all at once. Should only take two to three hours to max level if you are following a guide and have the funds to purchase materials you don't have.

The references to "gw2crafts.net" concern an online assistance service that functions like an add-on program. The "api key" is a code that identifies the particular avatar and allows the system to access data such as the resources and virtual money in the avatar's inventory.[38] The *Guild Wars 2* wiki defines it thus: "An API key is a code players can generate in their account settings that can allow third-party apps to access certain account data via use of the API."[39] Belonging to a well-developed guild of players confers a statistical advantage, called a *buff*, and some items in the game also improve crafting speed or quality of results.

The participants in the discussion suggest very different strategies for advancing a crafting skill. The player in Indonesia argues that the benefit to the character of crafted products is most significant at the highest quality levels, so there is no point crafting early on. The player in Romania apparently feels differently, perhaps considering crafting to be valuable in its own right, whether as a fun activity or for the levels of regular experience it can provide. The player whose location could not be determined suggests assembling all the needed materials, and a good deal of virtual

---

[38] gw2crafts.net/cooking.html

[39] wiki.guildwars2.com/wiki/API:API_key

money with which to buy more, then concentrating on the crafting until it has been completed, rather than doing it piecemeal. Similar alternatives may exist for local manufacture in the future real world, and different people may follow personally attractive strategies.

Conclusion

The 30 examples of MMOs were selected largely because they cover the two decades of this new online social form and because they exhibit much variation in social structure and the ways in which manufacturing is simulated. As reported in other research studies, I have explored about 25 more MMOs that were of interest for other reasons and will not be mentioned here. As the statistics in Table 2.3 indicate, the popularity as well as age of these 30 MMOs varies considerably, but that does not mean that old and unpopular cases deserve less attention. Often the least popular games were more experimental, thus offering interesting ideas that might be valuable in real-world distributed manufacturing, although not as exciting for action-oriented game players. For example, at their peaks *World of Warcraft* had about 10,000 times as many players as *A Tale in the Desert*, yet *Tale* has a vastly more complex and cooperation-oriented manufacturing system. Before considering overarching issues like communication and social structure, we need to understand the practical details of making things in virtual worlds.

CHAPTER 3

Principles of Virtual Manufacturing

The 30 MMOs studied for this project differ in how detailed the process of manufacturing is, how much effort is required, and how advantageous it is to work in partnership with other players. None can perfectly simulate real-world work, for example, the hand motions required to tie a string on an archer's bow, but that may not be a significant disadvantage because few local workshops of the future will be producing bows and arrows. It is the general principles that may possibly transfer from these online simulations to real-world applications, whether directly or by stimulating thought in new directions. One interesting abstraction is the issue of proportionality, a word that had mathematical as well as sociolegal meanings. What fraction of the total population will engage in local manufacture? What fraction of their time will be devoted to this activity and will receive what fraction of the total rewards?

We shall gain a sense of the practical experience of virtual crafting by looking closely at examples clustered in three sections. First, comparison of two games based on the same mythos from literature and the movies will consider the historical development of human industry from the dawn of time: *Conan Exiles* and *Age of Conan*. Second, a sense of the nature of production-centered virtual worlds is gained by considering a fantasy game that replicates medieval European society, *Shroud of the Avatar*, and two explicitly historical virtual worlds, *A Tale in the Desert* and *Pirates of the Burning Sea*. Third, *EverQuest II* will demonstrate how complex a virtual production system can become.

Two Simulations of Technologies from the Human Past

A pair of multiplayer online games based on the action fantasy fiction of Robert E. Howard (1906–36), *Conan Exiles* and *Age of Conan*, provides excellent environments in which to consider the historic development of human manufacturing technologies. Launched in 2018, *Conan Exiles* is a *survival game*, which Wikipedia defines as "a subgenre of action video games set in a hostile, intense, open-world environment, where players generally begin with minimal equipment and are required to collect resources, craft tools, weapons, and shelter, and survive as long as possible."[1] Social life and economic exchange are constrained by the fact that the players are distributed across hundreds of servers, each with a population limited to 10 to 50 players, depending on how it was set and whether it is a public or private server, a structure that some other very recent games have experimented with, each world being geographically rather small. Launched a decade earlier in 2008, *Age of Conan* is a classic massively multiplayer role-playing game, comparable to *Lord of the Rings Online*. Both technology and social structure are very primitive in *Conan Exiles* but advanced in *Age of Conan* where a rather big city named Tarantia is at least as large as and more complex than Bree in *Lord of the Rings Online*.

Robert E. Howard was a member of a loosely connected group of horror and fantasy writers that included H.P. Lovecraft and Abraham Merritt, perhaps the least academic of that trio but equally fascinated by the mysteries of the human past as reflected by ancient history and archaeology.[2] His main fantasy character, Conan the Cimmerian, was popularized to later generations through a pair of motion pictures in which the future governor of California, Arnold Schwarzenegger, played the title character: *Conan the Barbarian* in 1982 and *Conan the Destroyer* in 1984.[3] Both Conan games were created by the Norwegian game company, Funcom, which back in 2001 had launched the extremely innovative *Anarchy Online*, which Wikipedia says "was the first in the genre to include a science-fiction setting, dynamic quests, instancing, free trials, and in-game advertising."[4] Elsewhere I have argued that *Anarchy Online*

---

[1] en.wikipedia.org/wiki/Survival_game
[2] De Camp, L.S., C.C. de Camp, and J.W. Griffin. 1983. *Dark Valley Destiny: The Life of Robert E. Howard*. New York, NY: Bluejay.
[3] en.wikipedia.org/wiki/Conan_the_Barbarian
[4] en.wikipedia.org/wiki/Anarchy_Online

was also remarkable for its juxtaposition of competing ideologies about the future of humanity, in the context of what might be described as a war between capitalism and tribalism.[5] In adopting the popular Conan mythos, Funcom sought to gain greater popularity while retaining some commitment to intellectual sophistication.

Exploring the first 25 experience levels of *Conan Exiles* offline in a solo option allowed focusing on the technology of creating products. In a barren desert, one's avatar has been crucified and left to die, but Conan wanders past and frees it. The avatar must swiftly create protective clothing plus weapons and hand tools, then find water and food before dying of thirst and hunger. If one survives, the next goal is to find a good location to build a cabin and various equipment to produce the needed tools, weapons, and armor. At the time I explored *Conan Exiles* 2 months after its launch, a player's online post had suggested a location that proved ideal for the cabin, near a wide range of resources and seldom directly visited by wandering beasts.

Given that this was a survival game, the avatar could die of thirst. There were lakes near the homesite, but the avatar needed to be very careful about drinking from them, because alligators and hyenas were nearby. More slowly, the avatar could starve to death, and the first available food was insects gathered from nearby bushes, not the most delicious of foods. With care, eggs could be stolen from dinosaur nests. The chief food available was the meat of slaughtered animals, but the avatar begins the game without any kind of weapon, or even much clothing. Crude clothing that provided some degree of protection could be woven from plant fiber taken from the same bushes as the insects, but making tools required gathering the necessary raw materials and carefully crafting with them.

This is a standard feature of construction in computer games: Raw materials must be gathered before any goods can be produced. The ground around the homesite was strewn here and there with groups of stones and small tree branches, which could be picked up by standing near them and pressing the E key on the keyboard. The branches all looked identical, but the stones varied greatly. Pressing the I key would open the avatar's

---

[5] Bainbridge, W.S. 2011. *The Virtual Future*, 55–72. London: Springer.

inventory, where the stones and branches would pile up in two separate squares of the storage space, with the number in each pile clearly displayed. A section of the interface gave the user some currently available construction tasks, and selecting one for which the necessary raw materials were already in the inventory would allow making the product quickly, regardless of where the avatar happened to be at the moment. Combining five branches with five stones would produce a stone hatchet, capable of chopping trees and providing a little defense against animals, as indicated at the top of Table 3.1.

A better weapon is the stone club, which requires 20 stones rather than the 5 for the hatchet. Using these tools wears them out rather quickly, so the avatar must constantly collect more branches and stones, but putting too many heavy items in the inventory made it impossible to walk around. Thus, a key production item was a wooden storage box, which required twine made from the plant fibers and fully 100 pieces of wood chopped from nearby trees, a job that tended to wear out hatchets quickly. The campfire required 5 branches and 12 stones to build, but it burned wood, which required more tree chopping. Raw animal meat sickened the avatar, but it could be made safe by cooking. Almost every battle with a beast injured the avatar, and eating good food was the reliable way to regain perfect health.

One use for the wooden box was storing stones, wood, plant fiber, and twine that were needed in great quantities to build a cabin, which would provide safety from the occasional sandstorms and wandering alligators, as well as a place to begin manufacturing more complex things. For example, a wooden door used 5 pieces of twine (each of which was manually produced from 3 units of plant fiber) and 25 pieces of wood, whereas a sandstone doorframe required 3 pieces of wood and 18 stones. Once the cabin had been assembled, the next priority was the armorer's bench which could use animal hides to manufacture much better clothing than the plant fibers. The artisan's worktable seemed like a luxury, for example, used in taxidermy to prepare the head of an animal for display on the wall of the cabin, but it could also manufacture furniture once the avatar had invested in the proper training and had expanded the cabin. The tannery could improve the hides for even better clothing, and the carpenter's bench was especially useful for producing bows and arrows.

Table 3.1 Raw materials for initial tools that can be manufactured in a survival simulation

Tool	Application	Branch	Stone	Twine	Wood	Bark	Brick	Iron
Stone hatchet	Chopping	5	5					
Stone pick	Mining	5	5					
Stone club	Defense, hunting	5	20					
Campfire	Cooking, keeping warm	5	12					
Fish trap	Fish	10		5				
Wooden box	Storing items			12	100			
Artisan's worktable	Miscellaneous creations				40			
Armorer's bench	Crafting armor		240	20	160			
Tannery	Hides into leather		240	20	160	38		
Carpenter's bench	Carpentry		150		400			
Furnace	Smelting metals, stone		540					
Cauldron	Mixing concoctions			20				50
Blacksmith's bench	Shaping metal						50	100
Iron hatchet	Chopping wood	5						20
Iron pick	Mining	5						20
Iron mace	Defense, hunting							20

Here we have examples of manufacturing equipment that transforms raw materials into products, starting with the simple campfire: raw meat + wood = food. The most complex example in Table 3.1 is the blacksmith's bench, because making one requires 50 bricks and 100 iron bars, none of which can be gathered directly from the environment. First, a furnace must be made, at a cost of 540 stones, which require great effort to collect. Like the campfire it burns wood. The raw materials for each brick are 10 stones. Each iron bar requires only two ironstones, but none of them were available in the vicinity of the cabin. The avatar needed to explore, at great peril, eventually finding a good quarry for ironstones a significant distance to the northwest. Harvesting them required smashing big gray stones with a pick, which wore out quickly. Several trips were required to bring back enough ironstone not only to build the blacksmith's bench, but also to produce valuable products that were in every way stronger than similar items crafted at the top of Table 3.1: hatchet, pick, and club or mace. Completing the blacksmith's bench to manufacture metal weapons was like a local industrial revolution, opening a new phase of technological development for the player of *Conan Exiles*.

I originally explored *Age of Conan* rather thoroughly back in 2009, running four avatars that had different ethnicities and skills; then I returned in 2014 with one avatar to examine the changes that had been made since launch and to do an initial observation of the significance of guild cities.[6] In 2018, I ran an additional avatar for 165 hours in a highly promoted temporary instance of *Age of Conan* called Saga of Zath that operated only from January 24 until May 15, after which all the avatars migrated to the main server, named Crom. Like many of the most popular role-playing games, *Age of Conan* promotes cooperation by limiting the range of skills possessed by any one avatar. Focusing specifically on the sociotechnical processes to build a guild city, I selected architecture and weaponsmithing as the two crafting skills this avatar should develop, the other choices being alchemy, armorsmithing, and gemcutting. I joined a

---

[6] Bainbridge, W.S. 2013. *eGods: Faith Versus Fantasy in Computer Gaming*. New York, NY: Oxford University Press; 2016. *Virtual Sociocultural Convergence: Human Sciences of Computer, Games*, 60–64. London: Springer.

small guild, with roughly two dozen members, just big enough to have a serious city, but not so big as to rush to a quick completion.

The Conan mythos imagines an alternative past history in which lost civilizations and magical forces interacted with cultures similar to those the world really possessed a few thousand years ago. An avatar in *Age of Conan* washes ashore from a wrecked ship on which he or she was chained like a slave, on a jungle-framed beach not far from a city named Tortage which serves both to introduce the fictional world to the player and to provide a tutorial.[7] Unless the player uses a secret trick to escape at experience level 16, newcomers leave at level 20 of the 80 currently possible in this game and go to one of three ethnic regions. Conan himself was a Cimmerian, a Celtic tribe that qualifies him literally as a barbarian. However, he winds up ruling the capital city of Aquilonia, which resembles ancient Rome or perhaps Athens. The third original ethnic region was Stygia, essentially ancient Egypt. After the game's launch, a fourth ethnicity was added, named Khitan after an actual ancient nomadic Asian people, but apparently an amalgam of Chinese and Korean cultures. The ethnicities are not generally at war, and in ascending to the maximum experience level of 80 an avatar is likely to spend considerable time in lands belonging to each of the three original ethnicities.

The raw materials for manufacturing are primarily harvested from animals in the case of hides, and human enemies in the case of fabrics other than the most simple one, cotton, which can be harvested from a plant, and from trees and minable outcroppings of stone and metal. The guild my avatar initially joined built its city on the west edge of a region belonging to Aquilonia, named Poitain, that contained a full set of natural resources. Table 3.2 shows the system by which an architect could gather and transform the necessary raw materials into components that would be assembled in large numbers to create the city. Only after reaching experience level 20 could my avatar begin gathering the raw materials in tier 1 and complete a set of tasks to be ready to gather the tier 2 materials at level 50 and tier 3 at level 70. The crafting skills could not be learned until level 40, and similarly developed through stages. Weaponsmithing

---

[7] Ellingsen, E., G. Swan, and S.M. Halvorsen. 2011. *Age of Conan Manual.* Oslo, Norway: Funcom.

Table 3.2 The increasing difficulty of manufacturing more valuable architecture

	Tier 1	Tier 2	Tier 3
Gathering available at tier level			
Mining	Copper	Iron	Duskmetal
Prospecting	Silver	Electrum	Gold
Stonecutting	Sandstone	Granite	Basalt
Woodcutting	Ash	Yew	Oak
Crafting available at tier level			
Architecture	Ordinary	Advanced	Superior
A building plan	Parchment	Papyrus	Vellum
Component from mining	Brace	Lintel	Girder
Component from prospecting	Plain facade	Ornate facade	Grand facade
Component from stonecutting	Brick	Block	Slab
Component from woodcutting	Joist	Beam	Frame
Gathering actions required for architect workshop			
Mining	30	400	7,000
Prospecting	10	100	1,300
Stonecutting	50	1,200	15,000
Woodcutting	40	500	6,000
Gathering actions required for all city buildings (not counting walls, towers, gates)			
Mining	440	5,800	106,000
Prospecting	210	2,100	25,100
Stonecutting	800	15,200	188,000
Woodcutting	630	7,500	92,000

employed materials from three of the same gathering skills as architecture, not requiring stonecutting.

For example, to make bricks one must gather sandstone from an appropriate *node* or outcropping that can be seen on the computer interface map of Poitain. The avatar takes 3 whacks with a mining pick to get 1 unit of sandstone, and 10 units of stone are required to make 1 unit of brick. Note that "1 unit of brick" should not be conceptualized as merely "1 brick," but perhaps a crate full of bricks, and a rather large architect workshop requires just 5 of them in its most primitive form, the "50" in the table being the number of times the avatar must do 3 whacks on resource nodes. Two somewhat unpredictable events may occur after taking such an action. First, one may discover that the node has been exhausted, and no more sandstone is available there. Over time, the node will become fruitful again, but often the node one visits has already been harvested by another player, and little or none of the resource is available. Second, one's mining may be interrupted by an attack from a nonplayer enemy, who must be killed, gaining some reward in experience which the harvesting and crafting actions do not themselves earn.

When each of the many buildings in the guild city is first built, it functions at tier 1, and adding materials can take it to tier 2 and eventually tier 3. The small guild in the Saga of Zath server did construct all the buildings, leaving my avatar mainly to build the city walls, but did not invest the herculean effort required to take more than a couple of buildings above tier 1. When Saga of Zath was shut down, and the avatars moved to the Crom server, mine joined a well-established guild that already had 1,115 members and that owned a city in which all the buildings had reached tier 3. As Table 3.2 suggests, building an entire virtual city requires resource gathering by a large number of people operating avatars, thus somewhat realistic as a simulation of actual construction, at least as measured by the variable of human effort.

The crafting system in *Age of Conan* evolved over the years, but at present does not require that crafting be done while the avatar is standing at any particular facility. However, high-level products cannot be made unless the avatar belongs to a guild that has a workshop at the right tier in these professions: alchemist, architect, armorsmith, and weaponsmith. A city's tradepost does not automatically give the avatar new abilities, but it is a very useful center of commerce, with access to a bank, the player auction system, and various nonplayer vendor characters.

The center of the city is the *keep*, which Wikipedia defines thus:

> a type of fortified tower built within castles during the Middle Ages by European nobility. Scholars have debated the scope of the word keep, but usually consider it to refer to large towers in castles that were fortified residences, used as a refuge of last resort should the rest of the castle fall to an adversary.[8]

---

[8] en.wikipedia.org/wiki/Keep

A tier 1 keep increases the health of the avatar by 15 points, a tier 2 keep by 30, and a tier 3 keep by 60. These benefits do not require the avatar to be inside the keep, so the system expands the metaphor that keeps protect high-status people, perhaps implying that physical resources have indirect influence on members of the society. Similarly, the city's barracks, library, temple, and thieves' guild increase the variables that define the avatar's defensive and offensive abilities. This system illustrates how a simulation may be *implicit* on the large scale of gaining benefits from a guild city, but *explicit* on the small scale of chopping a tree or banging a pickaxe on an outcropping of metal ore.

Three Engineered Virtual Worlds

A perspective on some key issues in virtual manufacturing design can be gained by brief consideration of three diverse gameworlds: one recent fantasy, *Shroud of the Avatar*, and two unusual but illuminating historical simulations, *A Tale in the Desert* and *Pirates of the Burning Sea*. Bearing some similarity to the Conan games, *Shroud of the Avatar* is set in a quasi-medieval world, unusual in that it gives explicitly equal priority to manufacturing and warfare. In addition to making armor and weapons, players create or purchase glorious decorations to place in their virtual homes and castles. Advanced players and guilds can sell to others through nonplayer merchants of their own, which stand in some town's marketplace, rather than selling through a centralized, abstract marketplace as in most other MMOs.

At entry to *Shroud*, each avatar already possesses a few metal tools, which degrade only slowly in use. New ones can be bought, and kits can be purchased to repair old tools. Thus, a functioning technological economy exists from the very start, and it is based on a universal gold coin currency. The manufacturing skills are divided into three rough categories: gathering, refining, and production. Three of the five gathering activities involve the use of a specific tool on a natural resource: mining (a pickaxe on a metal node), forestry (an axe on a maple or pine tree, but not other trees), foraging (a sickle on one or another rare plant). Two others involve animals: field dressing (a skinning knife to remove the hide of a land animal after killing it) and fishing (a pole baited with a worm collected earlier). One of the six refining occupations, agriculture, requires costly land ownership, but the other five take the resources from one of the gathering professions and prepare them for a production activity:

1. Mining to smelting to blacksmithing
2. Forestry to milling to carpentry
3. Foraging to textiles to tailoring
4. Field dressing to tanning to tailoring
5. Fishing to butchery to cooking

In addition, blacksmithing, carpentry, and tailoring can salvage materials from some products either manufactured by the player or looted from defeated opponents. Note that tailoring appears twice among the production activities, using both cloth prepared by textiles and leather prepared by tanning. Table 3.3 shows how multiple forms of production combine to make some of the weaker forms of fortified clothing or armor, which provide at least a little reduction of damage during combat. Bolts of cloth are manufactured with a loom shuttle tool at a textile station, whereas the two leather components are made with a tanning knife at a tanning station, and metal bindings are produced by a smithing hammer at a blacksmithing station. Wax can be bought from many local vendors, whereas bone needles are rare and require a long trip to purchase.

Another production activity, alchemy, which is a romanticized form of chemistry, uses materials that do not require processing, but can be difficult to obtain. The two alchemy recipes my own avatar actually used often were *health potion*, which can be lifesaving during battle, and *recall scroll*, which can teleport the avatar home from a great distance. To create both, the avatar must be standing at an alchemy station, which looks like a chemistry bench, and have equipped a mortar and pestle. The ingredients for health potion included wax taken from corpses and garlic either found in the field while foraging or purchased from a local vendor, as well as empty flasks to contain the product which could be purchased from more distant vendors. In order to make recall scrolls, a recipe had to be purchased then "learned" (simply activating it in the avatar's inventory), as is the case for most advanced products. Prices for recipes vary, but a common price from nonplayer vendors operated by the game itself is 250

Table 3.3 *Materials required for tailoring three qualities of light armor*

Item	Bolts of Cloth	Leather Straps	Yards of Leather	Metal Bindings	Wax	Bone Needles
Cloth armor						
Helm	3	1			2	
Gloves	2	1			2	
Boots	2				2	
Augmented cloth armor						
Helm	4				3	1
Chest armor	9	2		2	4	1
Gloves	2			2	3	1
Leggings	6	1		2	4	1
Boots	2			1	3	1
Leather armor						
Helm			4		2	
Chest armor		2	7	2	3	
Gloves		3	1		2	
Leggings		3	5		3	
Boots			2		2	

gold coins each, which was what the recall scroll recipe for alchemy cost. However, it cost my avatar 700 gold coins to obtain the recipe to smelt gold ore, purchasing from the simulated salesman for a real-life player.

Among the most admirable and least popular gameworlds is *A Tale in the Desert*, which can also be described as one of the most socially desirable because it stresses cooperation among players, and does not permit violence. The "desert" in the title refers to the ancient Egyptian landscape, including Sinai and all the territory we currently call Egypt. True, the dimensions are smaller than the real lands, but still quite extensive, requiring hours to walk entirely around. Players can vote to open various chariot routes between specified distant points, providing swift travel, but at the beginning none of these exist. The fundamental concept is that starting essentially from scratch, the players must construct homes, production facilities, and eventually pyramids, creating ancient Egypt all over again, then ending the particular "telling" of the tale after a couple of years with ceremonies of mutual respect. The first telling began on February 15, 2003, and the eighth telling on March 2, 2018.

There are no real dangers in this virtual Egypt, so selecting a location for one's home is shaped only by the need to be near water and near a potential transportation hub such as a chariot stop or a crossing point of the Nile River. Walking along the shore, one may collect sand and mud, plus an occasional piece of slate. Skillfully banging two pieces of slate together can make a stone blade. Four pieces of slate plus one stone blade are sufficient to build a wood plane, but in use the blade must periodically be replaced, so it is good to have a supply from gathering much slate along the shore. Wood can be gathered from trees, then transformed into boards using the plane. Four boards can be assembled to make a brick rack, which requires three units of mud, two of straw, and one of sand to make six bricks. The straw comes from gathering grass and leaving it in bunches to dry in the hot Egyptian sun. Learning how to construct a compound, which can be a home or more often a building housing production machinery and supplies, requires learning this skill at an architecture school, after paying the tuition of 100 boards and 200 bricks.

Construction of a multipurpose building called a *compound* renders the avatar an *initiate* in architecture, one of seven disciplines. Strewn across the Egyptian landscape are schools and universities for the separate disciplines, which serve not only to train individuals in specialized skills, but also to unlock technologies for all the inhabitants of the area in a process called *research*. For example, at the branch of the University of Architecture in the Avaris region, as of August 2, 2018, local people had already contributed 22,276 of the 27,912 bricks required to make it possible to build crystal obelisks, but only 3 of the 308 required eyelet cut gems, and none of some other materials that they probably were not yet able to manufacture. Thus, many of the valuable products required not only specific raw or manufactured materials, but also great cooperative effort metaphorically considered as research, to unlock the ability to build the product. Advancement in each of the seven disciplines requires both individual and collective effort, with both competitive and collaborative qualities. Table 3.4 shows how far the Egyptians had gotten by August 2, 5 months after the telling's March 2 beginning.

The data were obtained from the public census records available at any University of Leadership, revealing first of all that the total population of virtual Egypt was only 684. There is little if any advantage to having multiple avatars in *A Tale in the Desert* because there are no limits on the combination of skills or property that one avatar can gain, such as those in *Age of Conan*. Table 3.4 reveals that only 6.9 percent of the 684 had failed to build a compound. The only discipline with fewer uninitiated Egyptians is discipline of the Human Body, for which initiation requires running around a fertile area identifying 35 different plants in 20 minutes, the first workout a player usually experiences after leaving a tutorial zone. After becoming an initiate in the discipline of the Human Body, the next rather fascinating task is learning and teaching acrobatic moves in exchange with other players, whereas the ranks in discipline of Architecture require building next an obelisk then increasingly more demanding structures, often in direct competition with other players. Like architecture, discipline of Art and Music required constructing physical objects, and many of the others include occasional manufacture. Construction materials become progressively more difficult to obtain, because mines and special manufacturing machinery are required, which renders many projects entirely dependent upon the cooperative groups called guilds.

An historical simulation of a more recent period is *Pirates of the Burning Sea*, which Wikipedia correctly says is "set in the Caribbean in an

Table 3.4 Progress of 684 Egyptian avatars across the seven disciplines

	Architecture	Art and Music	Harmony	Human Body	Leadership	Thought	Worship
None	6.9%	19.3%	16.8%	3.8%	16.8%	38.7%	42.8%
Initiate	62.1%	79.1%	59.2%	61.1%	76.5%	56.7%	35.2%
Student	17.8%	1.6%	12.7%	15.2%	5.4%	3.2%	15.9%
Prentice	8.5%	0.0%	6.7%	8.9%	0.7%	0.7%	4.4%
Journeyman	3.2%	0.0%	2.2%	4.7%	0.3%	0.6%	1.6%
Scribe	1.0%	0.0%	2.0%	3.7%	0.3%	0.0%	0.0%
Master	0.4%	0.0%	0.3%	1.6%	0.0%	0.0%	0.0%
Sage	0.0%	0.0%	0.0%	0.9%	0.0%	0.0%	0.0%
Oracle	0.0%	0.0%	0.0%	0.1%	0.0%	0.0%	0.0%
Total	100.0%	100.0%	100.0%	100.0%	100.0%	100.0%	100.0%

anachronistic 1720 and combines tactical ship battles and swashbuckling combat with a player-driven economy and open-ended gameplay. In the game, players can choose from 4 nations, Great Britain, Spain, France and the Pirates."[9] Anachronistic as some aspects may be, such as the display of a string quartet when that musical genre evolved only later in the 18th century, and the settlement of Bartica in Guyana over a century before it actually occurred, PotBS actually is rather authentic, and there is something glorious about building a sailing ship then cruising over to Port Royal to see the ruins from the "recent" 1692 earthquake.

Building a ship is not an easy business, vastly easier if one belongs to a prosperous guild that already possesses the necessary facilities. Many doubloons of money must be expended to operate a logging camp to provide the oak required for the ship's hull, and a warehouse is required for storing the many raw materials and manufactured components. Sawing the oak keel for a relatively modest "Corsair" Xebec ship must be done in a lumber mill, spending 105 doubloons, 10 oak logs, 3 iron ship fittings, and 1 keg of nails. Some of the materials could be bought from a simulated auctioneer at Bartica, but other essential materials required a dangerous sea voyage to obtain elsewhere. An especially big part of the cost was constructing a shipyard, which required

210 doubloons
50 oak logs
30 building stones
20 frame timber
100 fir planks
6 window glass
20 loads of bricks
2 pieces of oak furniture
14 oak blocks
2 lignum vitae blocks
6 kegs of nails
1 shop provisions for the crew

---

[9] en.wikipedia.org/wiki/Pirates_of_the_Burning_Sea

1 set of iron tools

plus every 2 weeks:

420 doubloons

1 shop provisions for the crew

The 100 fir planks were purchased for 3,200 doubloons at Rosignol, not far from Bartica, but the 15 fir logs appropriate to build the ship's mast required sailing 796 miles north of Bartica, to Orleans in the Antilles. The materials sold by the auctioneer had indeed been placed up for sale by other players, fellow guild members can be very helpful, and one must already be an experienced sea captain before contemplating getting into ship manufacture. The ships are simulated in great explicit detail, whereas the factories and warehouses are implicit and represented by windows in the user interface.

A Complex, Distributed System

Each virtual world's manufacturing system is somewhat different from the others, but an excellent example of fundamental principles is *EverQuest II*. Launched in 2004, on the basis of 5 years of experience with the original *EverQuest* that launched in 1999, EQII has been refined and expanded over the years. The main character I have used to explore EQII's exceedingly complex world called Norrath is a conjuror named Cleora, whose virtual life began on December 2, 2010, and by April 29, 2018, she had been operated actively for 327 hours. A second avatar, named Toynbee, added another 170 hours of exploration. At the end of her service, Cleora was primarily devoted to comparing the crafting professions in the public workshop immediately outside her simulated home in New Halas, the small city on Erollisi Island that serves as the social and economic hub of the archipelago in the Frostfang Sea. Both home and workshop are inside a cavern, entirely safe from the conflict raging outside, and near a tunnel that leads to oceanside docks where Cleora could quickly travel anywhere in Norrath.

Each *EverQuest II* character begins life in one player-selected *adventure class* in a system of 26, often described in terms of four archetypes: fighter, priest or healer, scout, and mage. As a conjurer, Cleora belonged to the summoner duo within the six-class mage archetype. Conjurors belong to the Good alignment, whereas the other summoner type, necromancers, belong to the Evil alignment, a cultural distinction derived from the original *EverQuest* game that will be described in Chapter 7. A conjuror can summon nonplayer allies that represent the four elements: earth, air, fire, and water. Note that fantasy gameworlds pretend to incorporate magic, but it merely means that poetic visual and verbal representations are used to communicate the actions of rigorous algorithms. Necromancers can summon zombie-like servants from beyond death, yet functionally that simply means these primary avatars can have secondary avatars exhibiting teamwork. All six classes of mages wear cloth armor, whereas scouts wear chain mail armor and the two other archetypes wear steel plate, leather, or chain mail depending upon their specific adventure class. This immediately suggests that classes will vary with respect to their interest in manufacturing armor of different types.

In addition to the adventure classes, there are *tradeskill classes*. These are learned after the avatar has begun gaining experience on adventures, and thus is able to begin harvesting raw materials from the dangerous environment, for example, the snowy wastes around New Halas that are populated with monsters as well as by an invading army of nonplayer characters. There are several steps in learning a tradeskill, as well as many tradeskill experience levels, comparable to the separate ladder of advancement that measures adventure experience. Over the years, both systems have evolved, most obviously raising the level caps that set the maximum for both kinds of experience. Avatars are not required to have tradeskills, and Cleora had not received her initial tutorial, learning how to make a simple candelabra, until she was already level 26 in adventuring. Given that her research task was exploring the fundamental principles of this virtual world, she gained adventure experience rather slowly, having reached level 88 in adventuring and only 30 in the sage tradeskill prior to the 2018 phase of the research.

Making a simple candelabra on December 11, 2010, required working at a forge, which could be found only in a few population centers where several manufacturing systems were also situated. One's avatar required only level 1 of tradeskill experience, obtained by taking on the *quest* or assignment called Forging Ahead, that was the first step in a seven-stage crafting tutorial. Before one could make any product, one needed to have learned its recipe, in early stages by receiving a recipe book and clicking on it in one's inventory to *scribe* it into memory. Also needed were raw materials, in the case of a simple candelabra consisting of two units of tin and one each of elm, root, and coal. The coal could be purchased from a nonplayer character called a *fuel merchant*, but the first three of these resources needed to be gathered out in the field from resource nodes of different kinds that were often situated in areas where one also needed to contend with dangerous beasts or other hazards. Prior to tradeskill training, an avatar would learn how to harvest, by gathering the following:

3 severed elm from logs

3 roots from clusters of roots

3 tin clusters from ore-containing rock

3 lead clusters from rock nodes

3 sunfish from schools of fish

3 jumjum from a garden or shrub node

3 rawhide leather pelts from animal dens

Whereas I took literally thousands of screenshot pictures while exploring inside the two versions of *EverQuest*, an equally useful source of information was the array of online instructions, walkthroughs, reviews, forums, and wiki encyclopedias. The tutorial shows how to operate the different devices used to manufacture products, which begins by selecting which recipe to follow, but is not merely a simple matter of loading the ingredients after that. Instead, one must watch the process carefully and be ready to perform the correct action to counteract different accidental errors that may occur, by swiftly clicking the correct icon or pressing the associated key. Here is how one of the preprogrammed crafting instructors explained this, as captured in one of my screenshots:

During the crafting process, you will sometimes see a warning icon appear in the area below the four progress bars. The warning icon will match one of your reaction art icons, and will have a name indicating the type of danger. The crafter can correct these problems by ensuring the next reaction art they use matches the icon of the warning. Successfully doing so will avoid bad things occurring (such as a loss of progress, or durability, or even injury to the crafter) and may also result in unusually good things happening (such as progress or durability gain, a skill bonus, or even the discovery of a rare harvest).

The tutorial requires making one product for each of the nine subskills, helping the player understand the division of labor and select the one subskill in which the avatar will specialize. They are classified as subskills, because from about skill level 10 to 20 the avatar will perform rather unspecialized manufacture within one of three skill categories, each of which leads to a choice among three subskills. For example, Cleora did the tutorial as an artisan, then the next 10 levels of tradeskill experience as a scholar, then chose sage as her specialty, rather than alchemist or jeweler that are also subskills within the scholar skill. At any time, an advanced crafter may change specializations, but that means dropping back to being a level 9 artisan, and losing all the skills above that very early level. Here are the seven steps of the tutorial that offer introductions to all nine subskills:

1. Tutorial: Forging Ahead
   • Craft a simple candelabra using your carpenter skills
2. Tutorial: Countering Problems
   • Craft a lead bracelet using your jeweler skills
3. Tutorial: Learning to Cook
   • Craft some jumjum cider using your provisioner skills
4. Tutorial: The Art of Weapons
   • Craft an elm greatstaff using your woodworker skills
   • Craft a tin hand axe using your weaponsmith skills
5. Tutorial: Scribing Scrolls
   • Craft a shackle (journeyman) scroll using your sage skills
6. Tutorial: Alchemical Experiments
   • Craft an essence of intercept (journeyman) using your alchemist skills
7. Tutorial: Essential Outfitting
   • Craft a tin chainmail coat using your armorer skills
   • Craft a rawhide leather backpack using your tailor skills

As is the case for many popular MMOs, an online service exists that allows one to look up individual *EverQuest II* characters one may have encountered, or guilds one may be contemplating joining, and that also serves to publicize one's own accomplishments. Called EQ2U and located at u.eq2wire.com it displays an amazing amount of information about each avatar, for example, whether or not the avatar had visited each of 1,008 points of interest in 44 geographic regions of Norrath. As of April 28, 2018, data about 3,029,131 avatars could be accessed, and with moderate manual effort I was able to assemble a dataset of their distribution across adventure classes and tradeskill subclasses, summarized for the total population and 5 illustrative adventure classes in Table 3.5. The method did not allow me to tabulate the number of artisans or early-career crafters who had not yet selected a subclass, but they are not significant in the distributed manufacturing system, and thus not of interest here. Fully 81.3 percent of the 3,029,131 had not yet learned a subskill, but this may realistically suggest what portion of a real-world local population would engage in professional crafting, approaching 1 in 5, keeping in mind that in *EverQuest II* this is part-time work, even though requiring semiprofessional experience.

For the population as a whole, the specialties are not hugely different in popularity, ranging from a low of 1.6 percent of the population for weaponsmith to a high of 2.4 percent for provisioner. MMOs vary in the extent to which an individual avatar would benefit directly from a particular manufacturing skill, in part because valuables such as weapons can be looted from defeated nonplayer enemies thus undercutting the value of manufacturing them instead from raw materials. A complex interplay of factors including luck will determine whether weaponsmiths can make better weapons than they can loot, their relative adventure experience versus tradeskill experience being an obvious determinant in *EverQuest II*. Some of the adventure classes have little or no use of weapons, whereas they all can benefit from the products made by provisioners. Thus, conditions in the marketplace can influence the popularity of a trade, as they naturally do in real-world economies.

The first two specific adventure classes in Table 3.5 are both fighters, but they differ greatly in popularity, so the 199,840 shadowknights would have greater influence on the economy than the 95,471 monks.

Table 3.5 *Distribution of avatars across tradeskill classes in EverQuest II*

Tradeskill Classes		All	Selected Adventure Classes				
Class	Subclass		Shadowknight	Monk	Fury	Wizard	Ranger
Craftsman	Carpenter	2.0%	1.8%	3.3%	4.4%	1.3%	1.9%
	Provisioner	2.4%	1.8%	3.7%	5.6%	1.6%	1.5%
	Woodworker	1.9%	1.3%	2.4%	2.4%	0.7%	8.4%
Outfitter	Armorer	2.3%	5.9%	1.0%	1.1%	0.3%	1.3%
	Tailor	2.3%	0.7%	6.7%	7.4%	2.5%	1.1%
	Weaponsmith	1.6%	2.9%	2.0%	1.6%	0.3%	1.1%
Scholar	Alchemist	2.1%	3.3%	4.1%	2.2%	1.1%	1.5%
	Jeweler	1.9%	0.9%	1.6%	3.0%	1.3%	2.2%
	Sage	2.3%	0.4%	0.7%	5.3%	3.8%	0.3%
Unknown	None	81.3%	81.0%	74.4%	66.9%	87.3%	80.7%
	Total	100.0%	100.0%	100.0%	100.0%	100.0%	100.0%
	Avatars	3,029,131	199,840	95,471	80,383	267,142	164,335
	Category		Fighters	Fighters	Priests	Mages	Scouts
	Armor		Metal plate	Leather	Leather	Cloth	Chain

Shadowknights use metal plate armor, which is produced by armorers, so that is their most popular tradeskill, 5.9 percent of them compared with only 0.7 percent for tailors who can make leather armor. The opposite is true for monks because they wear leather armor, only 1.0 percent being armorers compared with 6.7 percent tailors. This difference suggests that one very real motive for selecting a tradeskill is to make products useful to the particular avatar. Another motive is that using the product from a tradeskill gives information about the value of alternative designs, thus supporting marketability through more sophisticated expertise. Players often have two or more avatars, and they can freely exchange goods so long as their avatars are on the same Internet server, of which *EverQuest II* currently has 10, but 2 of them are testing servers not intended for regular use and 2 are intended primarily for European users. More significantly, most serious players belong to guilds, and they may avoid selecting a tradeskill already practiced by several fellow members, given that many guilds are cooperative sharing organizations.

The third adventure class in Table 3.5, fury, belongs to the somewhat ambiguous archetype called either *healers* or *priests*. Healing specialties are best adapted for team combat, in which the healer stands back while other team members engage the enemy, and prepares to reduce the damage suffered either by the entire team or by specific members that have drawn the enemy fire. But often avatars undertake solo missions and must have abilities that do not depend upon help from other players. Note that furies are more likely to have tradeskills than do the four others, distributed across specialties that can enhance the abilities of the avatar, including 7.4 percent tailors making leather armor and 5.6 provisioners, but also 5.3 percent sages who craft scrolls giving temporary combat abilities. Mages also slightly prefer the sage tradeskill, 3.8 percent of them choosing it, but they are less interested in tradeskills at all, 87.3 percent of them having no subskill.

Rangers prefer becoming woodworkers, 8.4 percent of them selecting this skill, for the simple reason that they needed to make arrows to shoot from their bows. However, the system changed over the years, as described well by a forum-poster, back in January 2014 in response to a question about which tradeskill a ranger should learn:

Up until a few months ago I would have instantly recommended woodworker as rangers went through loads and loads of arrows. They still do but it's been toned down to a single arrow per attack consumed so the consumption rate is dramatically reduced. It is still (as Feldon said in EQ2Talk) a bit like flinging coins at the monsters. However today the answer isn't quite so clearcut due to the arrow rate reduction and the advent of mass production. Depending on your server, I believe you can now pick up arrows at less than fuel cost compared to you doing a batch of 1 stack versus someone else doing a mass batch of 100 stacks which they then flood the broker with. If it's your only toon [avatar], I would still probably be inclined to do woodworker. Failing that provisioner as you'll always need food and drink.[10]

The reference to *mass production* deserves explanation. On November 12, 2012, an *EverQuest II* expansion named Chains of Eternity raised the level caps for both adventuring and tradeskills to 95, and apparently to encourage crafters to keep working made it possible above level 90 to earn Prestige Points that can be invested across three separate lines of advancement, one of which was mass production. It greatly reduced the time and effort producing up to 100 units of some product, but the avatar still needed to harvest or buy the necessary raw materials. In several other MMOs, as in *EverQuest II*, guilds can set up the equivalent of factories inside their private headquarters, and share among their members huge supplies of raw materials. This section will conclude with a description of the virtual layout of a public crafting area.

The workshop area in New Halas is somewhat more concentrated than some of the others in *EverQuest II*, because all the equipment and helpful nonplayer characters are near each other and not separated by trade in different buildings as they are in the large city named Qeynos. The equipment is arranged along a wall, from left to right: a chemistry table (for use by alchemists), two engraved desks (sages), a second chemistry table,

---

[10] forums.daybreakgames.com/eq2/index.php?threads/best-profession-for-noob-ranger.544895

a work bench (jewelers), a sewing table (tailors), a second work bench, two forges (weaponsmiths and armorers), a stove (provisioners), a woodworking table (carpenters and woodworkers), and a second sewing table.

Most of the raw materials need to have been collected from a wide territory and brought by the avatar to the workshop, but a variety of fuels can be bought on-site from Morag McMarrin, a nonplayer merchant. Every time an avatar gains a tradeskill experience level, Jalfa Eiskairn, the crafting trainer, is ready to sell the new level's book of recipes, for a moderate price. A few steps from her, Sana Strongbellow is ready to provide work orders that increase the rate of experience gain but require turning in the products rather than selling them. Not very much farther away stand Catherine Bowne, the banker, and Vald Jerngard, the broker. Bankers provide access to one of the avatar's storage facilities and, if the avatar's standing with a guild is sufficiently high, to the guild vault as well. Each avatar has a set of inventory bags that can be accessed anywhere, but the bank and a vault in the avatar's home can contain a far greater number of resources. The broker provides access to a player-to-player auction system, where not only raw materials but also advanced crafting recipes can be purchased. Each of these simulated human beings represents a different function and accesses a different part of the universal database, and they indeed represent roles real human beings would play in real-world distributed manufacturing.

Conclusion

The significance of gathering professions in the MMO economic systems may seem irrelevant to their suitability as simulations of real-world local manufacturing, yet it can be taken as implicit modeling of the fact that much manufacture requires assembling components from specialized sources, such as the metal hinges on the wooden door of a house or the buttons on a locally woven piece of clothing. More abstractly, we can predict that truly distributed manufacturing is not merely dispersed geographically, but also in terms of a flexible and fragmented division of labor. As greater fractions of the population enter the gig economy, many will combine multiple specializations, emphasizing different ones over time. This implies that their social networks and communication channels will also be dynamic and differentiated. The following chapter will show how online communications associated with MMOs can suggest the forms such future real-world communications may take.

CHAPTER 4

Modes of Work-Related Communication

Users of virtual worlds communicate with each other both inside and outside the simulated environments. There are essentially always multiple internal forms of text communication, including delayed communication e-mail and multiple real-time chat channels devoted to different numbers and categories of people. Whereas a few MMOs offer internal voice communication, typically external voice channels are used, such as Skype, Mumble, or Discord. Videos of action episodes are often shared online, not merely through static systems such as YouTube, but also streamed in real time over Twitch, in which the visual scene shows the perspective of one person, but others can also contribute voice and text. Essentially every virtual world has its own external text-based forums, as well as "subreddits" on Reddit. But a very important medium through which participants share valuable information is wikis, and most MMOs have their own separate wikis on Wikia.

By realistic analogy, future local communities will employ a wide range of computer-based communication systems, each optimized for a particular set of purposes. Given the wide range of personal goals and social structures enacted in multiplayer games, some fraction of ludic communications will be reasonably good simulations of real-world interactions, using comparable technology. An important observation is the fact that communications relating to the collection of materials and manufacture of virtual goods tend to be via text and asynchronous, whereas combat communications take place in real time and often by voice. The obvious reason is the pressure of time in violent action-related scenes, whereas manufacture is slower and often requires careful discussion of alternative solutions to problems.

Virtual History and Mentoring

With few exceptions, collective action scenes in MMOs take place in very limited virtual spaces, and are concentrated in time as well. From its 2004 launch, many missions in *World of Warcraft* required teams of up to five avatars, and the system could instantly connect the members, not merely in a separate text chat, but also providing them with updated information about the condition of each, for example, so that help could be provided to any member who was in trouble. Larger groups called *raids* could combine 40 avatars, in a hierarchical arrangement of 8 subgroups of 5. The fact that members were distributed across a relatively small space meant that they could usually see each other, even with their names displayed over the heads of the avatars and bar graphs representing the degree of damage they had suffered, thus expanding visually upon the text chat which tended to be monopolized by team leaders. Very early on, groups of friends began using voice chat in parallel, as illustrated by a famous video satire dating from 2005, as described in the Wikipedia page for its central avatar, Leeroy Jenkins:

> The video features a group of players discussing a detailed battle plan for their next encounter while Leeroy is away from his computer, preparing a plate of chicken. This plan is intended to help Leeroy obtain a piece of armor from the boss monsters, but is ruined when Leeroy himself returns and, ignorant of the strategy, immediately rushes headlong into battle shouting his own name in a stylized battle cry ["Leeeeeeeeeeeeeeroy!"]. His companions rush to help, but Leeroy's actions ruin the detailed plan and all the members of the group are killed. (Notably, the plan was already deeply flawed even before Leeroy ruined it, containing several critical misunderstandings of the then-current game mechanics.)[1]

In contrast, manufacture of products in *World of Warcraft* is an almost entirely solo activity, performed by a subset of players, typically when their friends are not online and thus there is less motivation to go on

---

[1] en.wikipedia.org/wiki/Leeroy_Jenkins

adventures. Only rarely while exploring more than 50 MMOs over a total of 10,000 hours did I observe players teaching each other in real time how to operate the manufacturing machinery. I only rarely saw text messages seeking advice about where to gather raw materials such as particular kinds of metal ore, outside of *A Tale in the Desert*, which emphasizes cooperation in manufacturing and where the locations frequently change. Usually that information is both stable and well documented on a game's wiki or forum.

The classic way to manufacture in *World of Warcraft* was to go to a city, such as Stormwind in the Alliance or Orgrimmar in the Horde, where specific types of production equipment were located within easy walking distance of each other, but not concentrated at a particular location. Near the equipment stood nonplayer characters (NPCs) who could sell hand tools and some materials to the avatar and provide the computational equivalent of tutoring in how to make particular kinds of things in a hierarchy of increasing difficulty. The chief form of communication between players, concerning manufacturing, took place at the nearby auction house, where materials and products could be bought and sold.

There exist two extensive *World of Warcraft* wiki encyclopedias, because of its great popularity, WoWpedia and WoWwiki. It is hard to know what fraction of the information on them was posted by players rather than employees of the game company, but they serve as advanced instruction manuals, for example, explaining every detail of all the gathering and manufacturing professions. Among the more interesting products I had written about before is the flying machine control, which allows avatars to fly in something resembling a helicopter over large factions of this virtual world.[2] One must be an engineer, having reached level 300 in that profession, as well as level 60 of general experience, and be an expert in riding. One must go to a remote location in Shadowmoon Valley and pay a non-player instructor 6 gold coins to learn the recipe. Actually making the control device requires assembling a variety of components, for example, 2 fel iron casings and 20 handfuls of fel iron bolts, which can be made from 26 fel iron bars, which were made from 52 units of fel iron

---

[2] Bainbridge, W.S. 2016. *Virtual Sociocultural Convergence*, 253. London: Springer.

ore that must have been mined or bought. The two wikis describe the product in almost exactly the same language, both referring to items in two predecessor games, *Warcraft II* (dating from 1996) and *Warcraft III* (dating from 2002):

> Flying Machine Control summons a gyrocopter-like flying machine. It seems to resemble the dwarven variant (as seen in Warcraft III) of the original gnomish flying machine (as seen in Warcraft II). It is a rare-quality flying mount available only to engineers and features two distinct modes: a hovering terrestrial version where the engines are stationed vertically, and an aerial mode where a horizontal propeller is deployed from the machine's chassis. If not moving and standing on ground, the gyrocoptor may randomly stop working and just smash to the ground. Similarly, if you are staying still while midair, the engine will fail and you will drop down a bit, but then restart within 4 seconds or if you move. This will not cause any damage to you, and will start working as soon as you move. The epic version of this mount is the Turbo-Charged Flying Machine.[3]

Wikis can be conceptualized as an *asynchronous* form of communication, because User A may post some partial information at one point in time, and User B may complete it later, even after several months. Thus, wikis have the potential to become historical repositories of information, lasting even long after the particular gameworld ceased to exist. One of the very best virtual worlds, *Star Wars Galaxies*, was shut down at the end of 2011 to make way for a competing game from a different company, *Star Wars: The Old Republic*. As of August 2018, a wiki for *Star Wars Galaxies* still existed. Its page for crafting said, "One of the unique elements of Star Wars Galaxies is that almost every usable item can be crafted by a player." It then listed these product categories: "Armor, Backpacks, Clothing, Droids, Food, Furniture, Harvesters, Houses, Medical Supplies, Painting Kits, Repair Kits, Ships & Ship Components, Spices, Vehicles,

---

[3] wowwiki.wikia.com/wiki/Flying_Machine_Control; wow.gamepedia.com/Flying_Machine

Weapons & Weapon Power-ups."[4] Players could even build factories that would automatically mass-produce desired products, if provided with the necessary raw materials. In an earlier book, *Star Worlds*, I listed the materials and components required to build a structure factory, a building that could make pieces that could be assembled into other architecture, such as wall modules[5]:

- Lode bearing frame and reinforcement:
    - 300 units of steel
- Body shell and casing:
    - 3 similar wall modules
- Structure foundation:
    - 250 units of low-grade ore
- Thermal noise and charge-proof shielding:
    - 400 units of low-grade ore
- Power supply unit:
    - 1 generator turbine
- Output storage unit:
    - 1 structure storage module
- Semi-automated assembly mechanism:
    - 1 manufacturing mechanism

As this list makes obvious, each large structure, including the structure factory itself, requires components that must have already been produced from raw materials and in many cases subcomponents. Indeed, building a structure factory requires wall modules, which themselves may have been products of already existing structure factories that belonged to other players and were either sold in the public market or donated to fellow guild members. Communication about complex systems like structure factories often included extra information, such as this from a wiki page:

---

[4] swg.wikia.com/wiki/Crafting

[5] Bainbridge, W.S. 2016. *Star Worlds: Freedom Versus Control in Online Gameworlds*, 92–93. Ann Arbor, Michigan: University of Michigan Press.

This structure can be used as storage, as items may be placed in the input hopper. However, the output hopper is not as accessible, only containing items the factory produces. Items removed from the output hopper may not be replaced.[6]

Players of *Star Wars Galaxies* could build and furnish complex personal houses, including a room where equipment to manufacture some products could be placed, and they could cluster them in towns managed by the local residents and possessing shared transportation and manufacturing facilities.

There are different ways to conceptualize the 2011 death of this marvelous virtual world. The successor *Star Wars* game was much more oriented toward prescripted stories, more like letting a player be a character in a *Star Wars* movie than living one's own life on one of the planets of the *Star Wars* universe. But *Star Wars Galaxies* had only a few tens of thousands of players near its end, and the wave of public interest in other freedom-oriented virtual worlds seemed to be receding at that point in the history of Internet. Users who valued freedom of action and technical creativity may have become explorers, spending just a few months in one gameworld before leaving to experience another. This suggests that some fraction of the future high-quality technical workforce may also be wanderers, going from gig to gig, or job to job, guided to some extent by online communications.

Beginning players could learn a crafting profession by using machinery in a public place. I can recall making a hovercraft vehicle at an outdoor facility, as avatars of other players walked past, in the public square of Mos Eisley on the planet Tatooine, not far from the cantina made famous in the first *Star Wars* movie of 1977. My virtual home included the machinery for making *droids*—as robots are called in the *Star Wars* mythos—some of which could be programmed to move along a predetermined path, perhaps distracting an enemy during a battle. As the archived wiki records, one of the most impressive professions was that of architect, which required considerable crafting experience (XP) even to begin:

---

[6] swg.wikia.com/wiki/Structure_Factory

Architect is one of the Elite Artisan professions that allow the creation of factories, harvesters, houses, furniture and player city structures. Many other professions are reliant on the Architect's abilities. Any player who wants a living structure bigger than a small house also relies on Architects. Houses and mining installations are the most popular crafted items, followed by factories for other Elite Artisan players. Sadly, the only Architect items that decay with use are lights, so the profitability of Architect depends greatly on new players and players switching professions. This profession requires 76 skill points to master, 29 of which go towards prerequisites. XP requirements to master, including prerequisites: 34,500 General Crafting XP (granted for crafting Artisan items); 1,408,000 Structure Crafting XP (granted for crafting structures granted in Architect)[7]

Four kinds of factories could be made in *Star Wars Galaxies*, each producing a different kind of product: food, equipment, wearables (clothing and armor), and structures (buildings and furniture).[8] A feature shared with some of the other most sophisticated MMOs was *experimentation*, the possibility to depart from the ordinary manufacturing process in hopes of discovering a recipe (called a *schematic*) for an improved version of the product. A rather extensive page on the historic wiki communicates the general process of experimentation:

> The draft schematic for the item you are creating may specify one or more properties upon which you can experiment. These include things like the base extraction rate or hopper size of a Micro Flora Farm or the number of hitpoints on a piece of Ship Armor. For each property, it lists which resource characteristics affect the value of the property and the effectiveness of your experimentation. To experiment on the item, you must select the Experiment option from the Finish Crafting Screen on the crafting tool, which then brings up the Experimentation Screen. This screen shows the

---

[7] swg.wikia.com/wiki/Architect

[8] swg.wikia.com/wiki/Factory

attributes and presents a horizontal line of boxes for each. You fill each box with one Experimentation Point until you either run out of points or decide to experiment with the current configuration (as long as you have the points, you can continue to run experiments). As you add points, the experiment risk may rise above 0; the more points you use in an experiment, the higher the risk but the higher the amount that the property will be improved on success (the best items are made with one big experiment that has a critical success).[9]

That wiki page offered much technical information and ended with links to four external web sources of further information. As evidence of the ephemeral nature of much online communication, two of them had this comment added: "Link doesn't work anymore, as of August 4, 2008." A decade later, one of the others had also vanished, but the fourth link went to a surviving British resource that offered both wiki-like data and forum discussions:

> The SWGCraft Project is an online community dedicated to helping fellow crafters in Star Wars Galaxies get the most out of their chosen professions. Apart from the friendly assistance you will get in our forums, you may also find our current resources database and our schematics database very useful.[10]

A sense of the value of forum discussions for understanding virtual manufacture can be gained from two surviving science fiction gameworlds, after which we shall briefly examine the communicative function of leaderboards in an historical simulation.

A Virtual World That Is Actually Real

There are many ways in which a computer simulation may fit into our real world. For example, a realistic simulation of the planet Mars could

---

[9] swg.wikia.com/wiki/Experimentation
[10] www.swgcraft.co.uk/dev/home.php

be used as a training environment for astronauts who would later visit that physical planet. *Entropia Universe* is real in a different sense, because it postulates a distant planet with rather more economic potential than Mars seems to have and it offers a system that allows players to bring their profits back to Earth. Wikipedia explains:

> Entropia uses a micropayment business model, in which players may buy in-game currency (PED—Project Entropia Dollars) with real money that can be redeemed back into U.S. dollars at a fixed exchange rate of 10:1. This means that virtual items acquired within Entropia Universe have a real cash value, and a participant may, at any time, initiate a withdrawal of their accumulated PED back into U.S. dollars according to the fixed exchange rate, minus transaction fees; the minimum amount for a withdrawal is 1,000 PED.[11]

It is theoretically possible but impractical to colonize one of the Entropian planets at no cost, so even a chance of profits requires investment of Earth currencies through buying PEDs. I extensively explored the original planet in this virtual universe, Calypso, over the years, and it remains the most significant. Its main website advertisement proclaims a vision of virtual reality:

> Explore Planet Calypso, the MMO-RPG experience where your decisions count for real in a stunning 3D-experience! Planet Calypso features a Real Cash economy and can be explored on all levels as an explorer, entrepreneur or in a number of other professions and roles. While hunters go after the indigenous species or the ubiquitous Robot menace that from early Calypso history on have threatened the planet, miners look for precious resources using seismic investigation methods and more. Some choose to craft tools, weapons and other items for the open market where Calypsians can both trade and invest. Others simply join for a

---

[11] en.wikipedia.org/wiki/Entropia_Universe

truly great Virtual World experience in a Sci-fi MMO setting. As a colonist on Planet Calypso all this is your world too![12]

Since 2004, the Engadget blog system has frequently posted Entropia news, usually positive in flavor, without easy means for checking the facts. The first brief blog, by James Ransom-Wiley, reported: "A Project Entropia player, known as 'Deathifier,' recently purchased the first-ever virtual island for $26,500 in an online auction."[13] The one cited source no longer exists. A year later, Ransom-Wiley reported that the virtual island had been bought from Deathifier for $100,000 by John Neverdie Jacobs.[14] In 2010, a press release proclaimed:

> First Planet Company, developer and publisher of Planet Calypso, the oldest planet in the Massively Multiplayer Online Game Entropia Universe, announced today that the largest Asteroid Space Resort property, largely known for housing Club NeverDie, has been broken up into smaller portions and sold off to new investors. The total purchase price for the parcels was $635,000.00 USD giving its original owner a stunning ROI of 535% in just five years.[15]

The Facebook page belonging to John Neverdie Jacobs says, "I place a lot of stock in Pursuing Dreams, enjoy synchronicity, Believe that life is a game, a very elaborate one. I Am My Avatar." As it happens, he and I are Facebook friends.

How real this game is and whether its dice are loaded cannot be resolved here. But players communicate extensively about production

---

[12] www.planetcalypso.com/index.xml?

[13] Ransom-Wiley, J. 2004. "$26,500 for a Virtual Island?!" *Engadget*, December 15, 2004, /www.engadget.com/2004/12/15/26-500-for-a-virtual-island/

[14] Ransom-Wiley, J. 2005. "Virtual Island Owner Recoups $26.5k Purchase Price." *Engadget*, November 10, 2005, www.engadget.com/2005/11/10/virtual-island-owner-recoups-26-5k-purchase-price/

[15] www.prnewswire.com/news-releases/planet-calypso-player-sells-virtual-resort-for-63500000-usd-107426428.html

and the economy in a forum devoted to the planet Calypso. For comparison, we can also consider Arkadia, a less populated planet in *Entropia Universe*.[16] Arkadia's website begins: "Welcome to a world of adventure and wealth. Join Thousands as they adventure into a world of hunting, mining, crafting and treasure hunting in a virtual sci-fi universe of possibilities."[17] Table 4.1 reports the activity to date in both planets' forums as of August 5, 2018. A post is an individual message, comparable to an e-mail message or Twitter tweet, and a thread is a series of connected posts usually about the topic of the first post. The table focuses just on the messages related to manufacturing activities and the more general economy, as classified by the forum system itself.[18]

One of the most popular recent crafting threads on Calypso began with a 665-word statement from an Estonian player, who had already posted more than 3,000 times, titled "Secret of Crafting."[19] Posted January 22, 2017, it had garnered 62 replies and 18,550 views by September 17, 2018. The Estonian's focus was on the complex and secret algorithms that determined the success of each crafting attempt, specifically the benefits of special limited blueprints. An online guide lists three somewhat random possible outcomes of a crafting attempt: "Success: The item you intended to craft, plus usually some residue and occasionally a new blueprint. Near Success: Some items may be returned and more than likely some residue. Fail: All materials will be lost and nothing returned."[20] Blueprints are required to make any particular product, in addition to the materials specified in the blueprint. Many blueprints are permanent, but as another website explains, "A limited blueprint can only be used for a set number of attempts."[21] Beginning players naturally assume that limited blueprints are inferior, and thus avoid them. But the Estonian explains how certain limited blueprints can be economically profitable, because they generate

---

[16] www.entropiawiki.com/Page.aspx?page=Main + Page

[17] planetarkadia.com/

[18] www.planetcalypsoforum.com/forums/forum.php, arkadiaforum.com/forums

[19] www.planetcalypsoforum.com/forums/showthread.php?291334-Secrets-of-Crafting

[20] universe.entropialife.com/Gamers/Guides/Crafting-Guide.aspx

[21] www.planetcalypso.com/guides/professions-activities/crafting/

Table 4.1 *Manufacturing and economy communications on two virtual worlds*

Message Category		Planet Calypso		Planet Arkadia	
Name	Description	Threads	Posts	Threads	Posts
Professions					
Hunting	Hunting tactics and strategy	8,414	183,851	210	3,080
Mining	Mining and resource gathering tactics, tips and equipment	3,986	93,417	137	1,943
Crafting	Crafting and manufacturing	2,514	32,728	93	1,032
Tailoring	Tailoring, coloring and texture for objects as well as clothing	129	2,758	44	321
MindForce	A distinctive resource that enhances abilities	704	11,783	7	53
Avatar beauty	Including hair styling, body and face sculpting	616	11,056	13	111
Taming	Gaining influence over tameable animals	658	10,468	27	331
Economy					
General economy	Overall prices and trends	3,600	104,199	84	1,314
Deposits and withdrawals	Real-cash transactions with Project Entropia Dollars	419	8,702	18	135
Land deeds	Comparable to stock in the operative corporation	187	7,825	15	403
Loot theories	Speculations about how various reward systems work	382	14,388	8	156
Trading	Items for sale, items wanted, price checks, services offered	86,169	679,185	2,354	10,004

unusually valuable results. Almost immediately, a novice asked general questions and received a quick reply:

Novice:

I'm not that into crafting but still have some questions
(a) How do I know minimum TT value of crafted item for any given blueprint ...
(b) How do I know average near success TT return for any given blueprint... before clicking that blueprint?
Also does these values have some easy to understand math behind or everything should be tested individually per each blueprint?

Estonian expert:

A you dont. So you have to test (as noone shares their results)
B you dont. So you have to test (i have done the test with achilles bps (all three) and many other bps). But it is actually the same as the average 90% return on every profession (or 95% as some claim). But with those bps i can guarantee you will tt profit
Each individually (thats why i keep it all in excel) so i can change material markups and so on.

Setting aside the occasional linguistic errors in these informal messages, they assume familiarity with the virtual world and some special terms used within it. Yet another online information website provides this essential information:

The TT value is represented by the nominal value carried by an item consisting of all component values included. This is the value that the game has attributed to an item. You can sell an item to a Trade Terminal and get the value the item carries.[22]

---

[22] www.entropiadirectory.com/wiki/tt_value/

When I did manufacturing on the planet Calypso, I always collected material beforehand, and then went to a production building in a main city that also had a bank, an NPC auctioneer for the player market, the right machine to build the product, and a nearby Trade Terminal, to which I could sell products if I did not want to use them or to struggle to sell directly to another player. The abbreviation "bps" stands for blueprints. Note that the experienced Estonian uses the Excel spreadsheet software to manually record data on sequences of important production attempts.

In the economy part of Table 4.1, the thread category called "land deed" deserves explanation, which Wikipedia provides:

> November 16, 2011—MindArk announced the sale of Calypso Land Deeds for $100 per deed. Each deed provides a weekly income to its owner, based on a percentage of the income that MindArk receives from running Planet Calypso and its other in-game areas (Crystal Palace and Space). March 26, 2014, Planet Arkadia announced a similar scheme to the Calypso Land Deeds. Planet Arkadia Underground deeds were priced at just $5 and provide a daily income taken from part of the revenue of Planet Arkadia.[23]

The Most Technologically Complex Virtual Worlds

An MMO simulating the distant future and one simulating the recent past reveal the potential complexity of near-future communication systems. *EVE Online* is widely regarded as one of the very most impressive virtual worlds—or virtual galaxies because it contains thousands of solar systems and primarily simulates spaceflight technology—offering many research opportunities and emulating many dimensions of real economies. The title of a 2016 collection of academic essays about EVE makes the key point: *Internet Spaceships Are Serious Business*.[24] My own chapter

---

[23] en.wikipedia.org/wiki/Entropia_Universe
[24] Carter, M., K. Bergstrom, and D. Woodford, eds. 2016. *Internet Spaceships are Serious Business: An Introduction to Eve Online*. Minneapolis: University of Minnesota Press.

of that book explored spaceship technology, especially investing time constructing a large number of different spaceships, some designed for battle and others for commerce.[25] In a section of my 2015 book, *The Meaning and Value of Spaceflight*, I explored what simulated space activities might mean to EVE players, by tabulating the goals listed in the in-game advertisements of 553 groups of players.[26] Most recently, in *Computer Simulations of Space Societies* I demonstrated how to mine asteroids for metals in *EVE Online*.[27]

The backstory reports that human space explorers discovered a nearby wormhole in space that allowed easy travel to another galaxy, which was quite suitable for colonization.[28] After a few colonies had been established in different solar systems, unexpectedly the wormhole closed, and the colonies fell into a Dark Age from which they have only recently recovered. Four distinct human civilizations now exist, in separate but relatively nearby solar systems, currently at peace, but differing in ideology and competing with each other. The area of the galaxy between these well-established worlds is called *high-sec space*, meaning that peaceful astronauts are relatively secure, because a universal police force named Concord will quickly punish anyone who breaks the law. Much of the galaxy is *low-sec* or *null-sec*, very dangerous and only guilds of players called *corporations* can function as police, but they tend to form alliances of corporations that are at war with each other. Some of the battles have been quite huge, with players vastly outnumbering the 487 attendance at the 2014 Weatherstock musical festival in *Lord of the Rings Online* or the 120 academics at my 2008 conference in *World of Warcraft*. In 2018, an *EVE Online* battle won an award from Guinness World Records:

[25] Bainbridge, W.S. 2016. "Virtual Interstellar Travel." In *Internet Spaceships are Serious Business: An Introduction to Eve Online*, eds. M. Carter, K. Bergstrom, and D. Woodford, 31–47. Minneapolis: University of Minnesota Press.

[26] Bainbridge, W.S. 2015. *The Meaning and Value of Spaceflight*. Berlin: Springer.

[27] Bainbridge, W.S. 2018. *Computer Simulations of Space Societies*, 148–56. Cham, Switzerland: Springer.

[28] Bainbridge, W.S. 2011. *The Virtual Future*, 113–30. London: Springer.

Fans of space-based video game *EVE Online* have helped set a new record after achieving the Guinness World Records title for the Most concurrent players simultaneously involved in a single multiplayer PvP videogame battle. A total of 6,142 players took part in an enormous battle—the Siege of 9-4—in January 2018 with the certificate being presented to the game's creators at EVE's Fanfest event in Iceland on Saturday (14 April). Produced by CCP Games, *EVE Online* is a space-based massive multiplayer online role-playing game in which thousands of players build ships, trade and, when the situation merits, go to war. It's particularly known for events such as the Siege of 9-4 where its legions of players get together in the same time and at the same place to take part in huge battles.[29]

Obviously, a great deal of communication over a period of months was required to assemble not only the fleets of spaceships but also the alliances of player corporations operating them. Each spaceship needed to be manufactured by players whose avatars had painfully acquired over time the necessary skills. The ships were of advanced types that required many complex components manufactured earlier, using a variety of sometimes rare raw materials. Much of the public communication about the manufacturing process, and the applications of the technology, takes place in the official online forums, so to provide some perspective Table 4.2 tabulates the numbers of communication actions in the most relevant sections.[30] The forum website is divided into 17 *centers* or message categories, 3 of which are reserved for all the messages in Russian, French, and German. The table shows data for four of these centers, collected in the first week of August 2018 and dating from as early as June 2017.

Each subcategory has its own contents web page, which begins with a simple introductory message, like this first one: "Welcome to PvP Ships & Modules: The place to share your thoughts on your favourite PvP ships, modules and fittings. Feel free to post your favorite PvP fittings,

---

[29] www.guinnessworldrecords.com/news/2018/4/eve-online-gamers-set-new-record-for-taking-part-in-a-huge-video-game-battle-522213

[30] forums.eveonline.com/

Table 4.2 *Communications relating to manufacture and use of space technology*

Category	Subcategory	Intro Views	Threads	Replies	Views	Passivity
Player-versus-player	Ships and modules	485	205	2,842	265,637	93.5
	Warfare and tactics	273	225	2,895	165,885	57.3
	Tournaments	525	66	680	99,370	146.1
Player-versus-environment	Ships and modules	641	378	6,405	695,380	108.6
	Missions	293	273	4,896	385,544	78.7
Industry	Science and industry	429	252	2,086	215,065	103.1
	Mining and extraction	537	242	2,919	285,509	97.8
Exploration	Known space	235	61	633	77,275	122.1
	Wormhole space	509	117	1,389	144,527	104.1
Total		3,927	1,819	24,745	2,334,192	94.3

guides and information in this forum category."[31] When the data were collected, that introduction had been opened and viewed by 485 people. The category contained 205 threads or discussions, on which people had posted 2,842 replies, and altogether the threads in this category had been viewed 265,637 times. The final column of the table is a passivity measure, calculated as the ratio of views over replies. Whereas warfare is a prominent feature of *EVE Online*, the table as a whole demonstrates that manufacturing the technology is a primary focus of communications, and players advise each other on how to handle the very complex systems for gaining skills and materials and achieving high-quality manufacture of advanced vehicles and components.

Some of the most popular threads in the science and industry subcategory are discussions of player-created software systems designed to analyze data and advise players on the best tactics to follow. As of September 23, 2018, there had been 9,165 views of a thread titled "EVE IskPer Hour Industry Program—Version 4.0," and 192 replies. Wikipedia's article about *EVE Online* explains the meaning of Isk in the title: "The in-game currency is ISK (Interstellar Kredits), which is also the currency code of the Icelandic króna, the real-world currency of Iceland, where the *Eve Online* development studio is located."[32]

Set 21,000 years in the future, *EVE Online* illustrates the extensive social, economic, and technological basis required to support modern warfare, and a far less popular but equally complex MMO has demonstrated the same principle for the real war that took place in Europe in 1940. As Wikipedia reports, *WWII Online* is

> a virtual battlefield, a combined arms war simulation. A player can command or crew a variety of accurately modeled aircraft, armored fighting vehicles, anti-tank guns, anti-aircraft artillery, and three naval vessels, or fight as a foot-soldier with a variety of infantry weapons. The game is played in real time alongside or against other players as German, US, British and French forces in a persistent world. Command structures and missions provide

---

[31] forums.eveonline.com/t/welcome-to-pvp-ships-modules/53

[32] en.wikipedia.org/wiki/Eve_Online

strategic and tactical layers while ranks provide a RPG layer by demonstrating leadership roles. WWII online uses a ½ scale map of Western Europe with 52,000 km² (20,077 sq mi) of accurate terrain (800 m resolution satellite data).[33]

Much of this MMO's complexity involves the mapping and related systems that facilitate organization of military units at particular locations, ideally guided by good strategies to outflank the enemy.

Players do not build their own tanks and aircraft, so crafting as we have seen it in so many other MMOs is absent. But they collectively assemble their equipment and themselves into armies that battle for weeks across the vast territory. Although the machinery is presumably manufactured far from the front lines of battle, players must develop general experience to earn the right to use a particular piece of equipment, plus specific skills that can be very demanding, for example, flying an aircraft. If I recall correctly, taking off in a German ME-109 single-engine fighter aircraft requires revving the engine just the right amount, because with its small wings the plane needs speed to get off the ground, but by the laws of physics revving the engine too much causes the plane to torque until a wingtip touches the ground, causing a crash. A *WWII Online* wiki says:

> Be advised that air combat is an incredibly complex field to venture into. Becoming an effective pilot requires long hours in the cockpit and countless fiery deaths. Do not be turned off by the steep learning curve however—once you get the hang of some basic concepts you will be ready to fight it out with the best of them. WWII Online has a good selection of various types of combat aircraft to choose from, all with their own peculiar traits, benefits and disadvantages. Aside from general similarities and the universal challenge of combat shared by all, each aircraft requires a specific modus operandi to ensure success. Learn by flying them all, offline, through reading and by experimenting, to find the aircraft and the practice that best suits your fighting personality.

---

[33] en.wikipedia.org/wiki/World_War_II_Online

First time pilot? Fly offline! If this is your first attempt at flying, we strongly recommend that you review the basic aircraft controls below and practice extensively offline before venturing out online. This is because aircraft availability online is severely limited and senseless waste of aircraft is largely frowned upon by your fellow pilots. Once online, do not hesitate to ask for help and advice— you will find many helpful pilots online who are eager to help you along.[34]

A main implicit mode of communication between players, which exists for some other war-based MMOs like *EVE Online*, is an online system of *leaderboards*, which are constantly updated systems that report the accomplishments of the players, often identified by name and described through statistics. *WWII Online* is episodic, replaying the war in a series of many *campaigns*, so the leaderboard statistics tend to report accomplishments in the most recent one. Around noon on August 25, 2018, the online database Consolidated Service Record reported that Campaign 155 was in progress, having started back on August 2.[35] It has a page for every active *persona* (persistent avatar), reporting that individual's activity during the campaign, and data about the highest-scoring players are compared on the Stats Wall of Fame. At that point in the campaign there had been 147,133 deaths, of which 139,750 could be attributed to a specific enemy solider and thus counted as kills. A player's persona does not die, only the current avatar of it, so these figures may be higher than the unknown number of actual people who played the game during this period. Interestingly, the public database reports which primary equipment avatars were using when they either killed or died. Table 4.3 summarizes the most relevant categories.

In 100,315 cases an infantry soldier was able to kill an enemy, probably with a rifle, and in 110,191 cases an infantryman was killed, whether by a foot soldier on the opposite side, a mortar shell, a tank, or a dive-bomber. The ratio of kills to deaths is 0.91, which suggests the relative weakness of infantry in comparison with soldiers benefitting from armor,

---

[34] wiki.wwiionline.com/view/Air_Force

[35] stats.wwiionline.com/sidesummary.php

Table 4.3 Leaderboard reports for a simulation of World War II

Weapon Class	Kills	Deaths	K/D
Soldiers			
Infantry	100,315	110,191	0.91
Paratrooper	648	734	0.88
Big guns			
Antiaircraft artillery	2,012	3,999	0.50
Antitank gun	3,693	5,657	0.65
Heavy mortar	630	892	0.71
Light mortar	453	930	0.49
Tanks			
Heavy tank	2,770	518	5.35
Medium tank	9,858	3,708	2.66
Light tank	4,935	1,632	3.02
Aircraft			
Fighter	4,278	3,064	1.40
Fighter bomber	1,562	860	1.82
Tactical bomber	940	497	1.89

as dramatically indicated by the 5.35 kills/deaths ratio for heavy tanks. But only a few tanks were available, and foot soldiers were necessary to take and hold territory. Such comparisons help players plan their investment of time, motivating them to gain valuable skills and master potent technologies. More generally, as an indirect mode of communication between people, leaderboards express prestige, motivate participants to increase their status, and provide some degree of implicit advice about how to achieve progress.

Building Virtual Worlds Within Virtual Worlds

A rare subset of virtual worlds, including *City of Heroes* and *Star Trek Online*, permitted players not only to manufacture products and build houses, but also to create new missions and areas of the game, which other players could experience. This takes communication to a higher level. *City of Heroes* launched its pioneering *mission architect* on April 8,

2009. Here is how Wikipedia described it: "The Architect release gave players the ability to construct custom mission arcs, with customized enemies and layouts that could then be played by all other players."[36] Among the very most beloved MMOs that were cancelled, *City of Heroes* has been the center of serious revival attempts, and much of the online communication has been preserved. During November 2012, the last month of its existence, a frequent YouTube poster using the moniker Elizibar posted videos of architect missions, a marvelous contribution to the history of virtual worlds. Table 4.4 lists seven of them, with their duration in minutes and part of Elizibar's written comments. The term "farming" in two of them refers not to agriculture, but to the practice of gaining loot and experience by killing vast numbers of nonplayer enemies, often in the absence of a motivating story.

Elizibar had created one of these architect missions, and several other players posted videos of missions they had themselves created. For example, Jodis Welch introduced an hour long video thus: "Heading into the final hours of the game, I am joined by some of my CoH friends as we play through my Mission Architect arc called Tower Demolition."[37] Another rather creative example was Apocalypse Cow, a 50-minute architect mission posted in YouTube by a person using the name TotalCowage, pretending that all the inhabitants of the city were actually cattle,

> recorded in the final few days before the City is itself about to be butchered for good. WATCH as the Bovine Avenger walks us through his finest hour, CRY as he points out all the ways in which un-addressed bugs which were added since 2009 break what once was then a perfectly honed Arc... And then feel really melancholy as this world closes for good... I hope it captures some of the creativity that was possible with the Mission Architect.[38]

After the pioneering example of *City of Heroes*, in 2011 *Star Trek Online* offered a sophisticated system called the Foundry, which was the topic of

---

[36] en.wikipedia.org/wiki/City_of_Heroes

[37] www.youtube.com/watch?v=G-46eMNnGPw

[38] www.youtube.com/watch?v=nTl21lTxB1k

Table 4.4 Illustrative YouTube videos of the products of mission architect

YouTube ID	Title/Creator	Duration	Test Comment by Elizibar
SYNCPTPUCMg	Two Tickets to Westerly by OPW	27 min	Set in King's Row, it's about one young man's struggle to leave the Skulls and start a new life with his girlfriend somewhere less poverty-stricken and crime-ridden
-lzpRVtmNQs	Nightmare in Paragon by ROBOKiTTY	33 min	Its tone is a bit different from other City of Heroes content, at least at the time, as it focuses on something more like "Survival Horror" than "Superheroes." That's not to say you don't get to be super in the arc, you do, it's more that the enemies exploit some of the mean things you can do in Mission Architect, like having more than one Radiation using enemy killing your defense in each group
MIjMqtta5gw	Project Carnival by Godspawn	23 min	We're tackling that hottest of issues in Mission Architect: Fire Farming. I'm not one of those hardcore farmers, but I do rather enjoy it from time to time. The fire farm in question is pretty simple: big map full of enemies to plow through, no ambushes or other gimmicks.
Pd9E17uhk2w	Strife of the Grave by Elizibar	28 min	Strife of the Grave is an old arc, made when Mission Architect was relatively new. I've had to fix it repeatedly as the developers changed things, which is a sad fact of life
CMzppiFh_q	Icebreaker Roboslicers by TopDoc	5 min	A now-defunct form of farming. Called "CEBR" (for Claws/Elec Brutes Rule) it's a sort of ambush farm where the player is dropped down to level 2 and forced to fight off multiple ambush waves at the same time. All in all I always found it a sort of frenetic button mashing goodness, but like all farming it got old very fast
G6m89_QyhW4	Villain Assault!! by Black Fin	17 min	When the Mission Architect was younger, I used to play a game I call "0-Star Roulette." It involves searching for missions with no ratings, flipping through the search list at random, and then just jumping in and picking one to play
pxGIY4CyTqQ	Crtl + Alt + Reset! by Bubbawheat	20 min	Time loops! They've been with gamers since at least the first Final Fantasy game, and they always seem to sneak back in. This arc is based entirely around a time loop, a malevolent time loop of doom

a chapter of my earlier book *Star Worlds*.[39] Several descriptions of how it can be used by players to create missions are available online. On September 22, 2018, it was possible to find and copy summaries of the in-game reviews of 101 English-language player-created missions, each of which had received at least 100 reviews. The format is in these parts: (1) the creator's brief description of the mission, (2) a graph of how many of the reviewers gave each quality rating on a 5-point scale, (3) a set of 8 categories to which reviewers could optionally assign the mission, and (4) a button named "View" that would open a list of any written comments that reviewers had made. Table 4.5 looks at distributions across the eight categories, in terms of high versus medium popularity and connection to the two main factions, the United Federation of Planets and the Klingon Empire.

The first six categories are pairs of opposites. Although missions often tell stories around combat, some tell nonviolent tales whereas others are narrationless battles. In space, the player is usually represented by a ship with virtual crew, whereas on the ground of a planet their avatars look like people, but missions can combine multiple locations. Some missions are composed around the actions of a single player, who operates solo, whereas other missions require fighting multiple enemies and thus require a group. The puzzle category seems reserved for very intellectual challenges.

The term "quarters" refers to what is essentially a virtual home. Around 2014 this message spread throughout the STO player community: "It is now possible to tag projects as category Quarters, for your entire player housing and crew quarter's needs."[40] The quarters category is best represented by the mission Apartment on Bajor by a player using the moniker number 158, who offered this description:

> My custom made apartment on Bajor, Now contains a Day and Night map with working like objects (thank you Tacofangs!). Part of Starbase UGC's Player Housing Project. No mission, just

---

[39] Bainbridge, W.S. 2016. *Star Worlds: Freedom Versus Control in Online Gameworlds*, 186–210. Ann Arbor, Michigan: University of Michigan Press.
[40] www.reddit.com/r/sto/comments/2d10es/playing_housingquarters_tags_coming_to_the_foundry

Table 4.5 *Classification of foundry missions by reviewers*

Characteristic Categories	All Reviews	Popularity		Faction	
		High	Medium	Federation	Klingon
Story	23.0%	23.3%	18.8%	23.2%	21.9%
Combat	23.5%	23.6%	23.0%	23.2%	24.8%
Space	20.4%	20.8%	16.0%	20.5%	20.2%
Ground	14.6%	14.1%	20.7%	14.2%	16.3%
Solo	11.9%	11.6%	15.6%	11.8%	12.2%
Group	2.3%	2.3%	2.0%	2.3%	2.1%
Puzzle	3.0%	3.1%	2.0%	3.3%	1.6%
Quarters	1.3%	1.3%	2.0%	1.4%	0.9%
	100.0%	100.0%	100.0%	100.0%	100.0%
Categorizations	177,925	165,103	12,822	145,489	32,436
Missions	101	50	51	65	36

a map. Enjoy. Entrance located on Bajor, in the building across from the Fountain.

The term *map* refers to a distinct virtual environment, and two or more maps can be connected in a mission. Of the 210 players who reviewed this apartment, 151 loved it, and 75 categorized it as quarters.

Interpreting the numbers in Table 4.5 cannot be conclusive, especially because many reviewers fail to mark categories, whereas others quite appropriately mark several for each review. The total number of categorizations—the sum of all the categories checked across all the reviews in the sample—was 177,925, but the number of reviews was 361,852. Given the ability to assign a mission to several categories, this means that fewer than half of the reviewers bothered to categorize. But we do see some interesting patterns, especially when comparing the 50 high-popularity missions that received at least 1,000 reviews each with the medium popularity missions that got between 100 and 999 reviews each. Having a story and taking place in space seem to be attractive features of more popular missions. Here popularity is defined as the number of reviews, which measures how many players undertook the mission, not the reviewers' ratings of mission quality. On the 5-step scale in which 5 means "loved it" and 1 means "did not like it," the high-popularity missions actually rated only slightly higher, 4.3 compared with 4.2 for the medium-popularity missions. Older missions will have had more time to get reviewed, and several factors may attract players to a mission, including whether the inscrutable game managers qualify the mission for special rewards and whether the creator of the mission belongs to a large and influential *fleet* (guild) of players.

Conclusion

We might naturally imagine that communication between workers in real-world local manufacturing will take place face-to-face, and certainly some of it will. However, my experience decades ago as a piano tuner and repairman provides a deeper perspective.[41] People with this highly

---

[41] Bainbridge, W.S. 2014. *Personality Capture and Emulation*, 112–17. London, UK: Springer.

technical craft in medium-sized towns had little if any direct contact with others who do the same work, but primarily shared advice through the Piano Technician's Guild by written letters or telephone calls, and today that organization has an online presence.[42] More common were personal visits to the local piano store, but much of the communication with the store about new customers for the tuner took place by telephone. The work was done largely in customer's homes, but arranged by telephone, and some work was done in the tuner's own workshop, where it was also possible to build musical instruments of simpler types than pianos. Replacement parts needed to be bought from a small number of suppliers in distant cities, but occasionally some specialized task would be hired out to a different professional who lived in town. An excellent historical example of distributed manufacturing is the predecessor of the piano, the harpsichord, which was built in independent workshops in cultural centers, that used a variety of raw materials and components provided by other local and long-distance suppliers, for example, the wires that produced the musical tones.[43] Whatever the exact fraction, communications to and from local workshops in future will often be text-based and asynchronous in this era of Internet, just as in MMOs.

---

[42] www.ptg.org/

[43] Bainbridge, W.S. 2012. "Harpsichord Makers." In *Leadership in Science and Technology*, 746–53, ed. W.S. Bainbridge. Thousand Oaks, California: Sage.

CHAPTER 5

Socio-economic Structure and Dynamics

The social and economic systems of a virtual world tend to overlap significantly, but not to be identical. Typically, as, for example, in *World of Warcraft*, pairs of individual avatars may be "friends," which means they can notice when a friend comes online and can easily set up a private chat. Essentially every MMO supports persistent groups, typically called *guilds*, in most cases allowing an avatar to belong to only one, such that each group should develop loyalty and social cohesion. Within a guild, players may exchange virtual products, as gifts, as barter items, or by selling for the virtual currency used within this particular virtual society. In most cases, there also exists an automated auction house, through which strangers may buy and sell items. But much of the economy involves buying and selling between a player's avatar and automatic non-player character (NPC) simulated people. Comparison of the systems in different MMOs can offer insights into how to set the parameters for support of social relations, and development of a vigorous local economy, in real-world communities.

The skills and material resources used by artisans in manufacturing are associated in a myriad of ways with other features of technological society. As we saw in Chapter 2, a pair of avatars in *Lord of the Rings Online* could profit from a very strict division of labor, in which a key part of the structure was the raw materials required for production of particular goods. We cannot yet be sure what range of products will be produced by local manufacturing, yet presumably many of them will be made by small workshops with a small staff. This implies that skill specialization will develop under conditions very different from mass production, in which the number of employees is large enough to include many highly specialized workers. Some expertise can now be offloaded on computers, but it will often be necessary for one person in a local workshop to possess multiple skills. Alternately, some individuals will be highly specialized but work only part-time in their specialty, perhaps in what has come to be called the *gig economy*.

Structural Division of Labor

Massively multiplayer role-playing games differ greatly in the significance they invest in virtual manufacture and in how it is organized. *World of Warcraft* is an example of a relatively simple and rigid system, in that it allows each avatar to participate in only two of the main gathering and production activities, supplemented with a few minor occupations that any avatar may practice. Here we can get a clear picture of the system with decade-old data I collected on January 12, 2008, on two contrasting Internet servers, Emerald Dream that was designed to emphasize player-versus-player combat, and Scarlet Crusade that was not.[1] Using an add-on program called CensusPlus, I captured data on the 1,517 avatars active that day, sampling hourly over a period of 16 hours. Only 54 of them practiced none of the main professional skills, 83 practiced 1, and 1,380 practiced 2 skills. Of this last group, 130 had two gathering skills, which implied they were collecting resources simply to sell, or to give to a second avatar of the player which specialized in production, or to share with a guild. Table 5.1 tabulates the specialties of the 1,019 avatars that practiced 1 gathering skill and 1 production skill.

As avatars travel across the virtual landscape, they encounter two kinds of *nodes* from which resources can be peacefully gathered, plants from which herbs can be taken, and metal outcroppings that can be mined. After killing many kinds of animals, an avatar with the right skill and tool can skin off the leather hide. So, the three gathering skills in WoW are herbalism, mining, and skinning. Table 5.1 clearly shows that herbalism provides the raw materials for the fanciful form of chemistry called alchemy, whereas skinning provides the raw material for leatherworking. The situation for mining is more complex, because three forms of production require the materials it can gather: blacksmithing, engineering, and jewelcrafting. Note that far more of the avatars practice mining, given

---

[1] Bainbridge, W.S. 2000. *Online Multiplayer Games*, 68–73. San Rafael, California: Morgan and Claypool.

the bigger market it serves. In second place is skinning, somewhat more popular than herbalism, perhaps because every avatar needs to kill animals from time to time and can profit from being able to skin the hides off them.

The majority of the avatars in Table 5.1 practice the gathering skill that supplies materials for their own production skill. This raises the question of how social their players are, rather than experiencing *World of Warcraft* solo. Yet combining two skills that harmonize well with each other can increase the level of performance of both. This is true because we are really talking about two very different definitions of skill: (1) the ability of the avatar to perform a particular gathering or production activity at an increasing level of difficulty and (2) the knowledge possessed by the player that supports good decisions about what actions to take, such as gathering materials for a particular product that can sell for a high price in the marketplace.

Depending upon the particular MMO, an avatar can gain production-related skills in primarily four ways: (1) by practice, repeatedly performing the same skill-related action; (2) indirectly by gaining general experience that can raise a limit set on the skill or offer access to territories from which more advanced materials can be gathered; (3) by purchasing and using *recipes* or *schematics*; and (4) by receiving explicit training from specialized NPCs. A similar diversity of routes to progress may exist in

Table 5.1 Skill combination in a census of 1,019 World of Warcraft avatars

Production skill	Gathering skill		
	Herbalism	Mining	Skinning
Alchemy	89.9%	0.4%	0.0%
Blacksmithing	0.0%	32.7%	1.4%
Enchanting	4.4%	8.8%	8.9%
Engineering	0.4%	31.7%	1.7%
Jewelcrafting	0.4%	22.5%	1.0%
Leatherworking	0.0%	0.2%	78.2%
Tailoring	4.8%	3.6%	8.9%
Total	100.0%	100.0%	100.0%
Avatars	228	498	293

the future work of distributed manufacturing, but there may also be government regulations or professional standards set by occupation-specific
organizations, comparable to the *World of Warcraft* limit of two tradeskills.
MMOs probably do not simulate all the factors that will operate in the
real world, but comparing several of them can highlight issues that need
to be considered.

Lord of the Rings Online imposes a level of structure above the separate
professions, calling it *vocations*. As described in Chapter 2, each vocation is a combination of three professions. A player may select a vocation for an avatar, but cannot freely select professions. Apparently, the
game designers developed this complex system in order to balance solo
and social dimensions. To get a sense of the structure of this division of
labor, Table 5.2 reports numbers of avatars in each vocation and profession from a dataset that will be analyzed differently in a future publication, from a sample of 2,452. The full dataset was collected by examining
every manufactured item for sale in the public market in each of the 10
LotRO servers, but here leaving out the unusual Brandywine server where
very extensive sales of high-level manufactured items required a different method of analysis. Seeing the market on a particular server requires
having an avatar on it, positioned in an auction hall. Many items for sale
had been collected, often in combat with an NPC, but manufactured
items were clearly labeled as such because they displayed the names of the
avatars who created them. The name of the avatar who posted the item
on the market was often different, either an alt of the player whose other
avatar made the item, a sales representative for that avatar's guild, or even
the avatar of a player who bought items cheap in hopes of selling them for
a higher price. I even saw cases in which an avatar had been moved from
one server to another, at some dollar cost, in order to transport items to a
market that would pay higher prices in the game currency.

A page of a LotRO wiki titled Crafter Interdependence correctly
reports:

> Many of the crafting Professions are interdependent, or more cor-
> rectly, dependent on a particular Profession other than their own.
> This feature of the crafting system is by design and is intended to
> foster development of the crafting community. It is common for

Table 5.2 Numbers of avatars having the given trio of professions in their vocation

Professions	Armorer	Armsman	Explorer	Historian	Tinker	Woodsman	Yeoman	Sum
Gathering								
Farmer				572		291	162	1,025
Forester			418			291		709
Prospector	315	193	418		501			1,427
Production								
Cook					501		162	663
Jeweler					501			501
Metalsmith	315							315
Scholar				572				572
Tailor	315		418				162	895
Weaponsmith		193		572				765
Woodworker		193				291		484

Production Professions to be dependent on Gathering Professions. For example, a Metalsmith relies on a Prospector to gather Ore and refine it into metal bars that are essential for metalsmithing.[2]

Metalsmiths happen to be one of the three professions found in only one of the vocations, in this case armorer, the first column of data in the table. They can make shields, armor, and tools, all of which require metal ingots, which the prospector profession can provide.[3] Therefore, an armorer can accomplish much of metalsmithing without collaboration with another avatar, because all metalsmiths are also prospectors. However, the tailor profession that is also included in the armorer vocation requires materials that can be provided only by foresters, so it pushes an armorer to connect to other avatars and players, or at least to be active in the marketplace. There are 315 armorers in the table, so also 315 metalsmiths. But both prospector and tailor professions belong to more than one vocation, so their numbers are higher, 1,427 and 895, respectively. In Chapter 2, we already mentioned the jeweler profession, which also belongs to only one vocation.

The scholar profession, possessed only by the 572 historians, has some of the qualities of gathering as well as producing:

> A Scholar requires a Scholar's Glass in order to study relics, texts, carvings and trinkets from days gone by. The Scholar can find these items by using the Track Artifacts skill, which directs him to the nearest Artifact in the world around him. Once he has studied the Artifact sufficiently, the scholar may then combine the knowledge he has gained with components purchased from a Novice or Expert Scholar vendor, to craft a new, useful item. A number of advanced recipes requires Crafting Rare Components.[4]

Scholars can make master journals that improve the productivity of other professions, including metalsmiths and tailors. Both metalsmiths

---

[2] lotro-wiki.com/index.php/Crafter_interdependence
[3] lotro-wiki.com/index.php/Metalsmith
[4] lotro-wiki.com/index.php/Scholar

and tailors can make armor, but of different kinds for avatars belonging to various adventuring classes. Metalsmiths use metal to make heavy armor for guardians, captains, and champions. Tailors make light armor that any class may use and medium armor from cloth and leather. Lore-masters, minstrels, and rune-keepers are limited to light armor. Metalsmiths and tailors produce armor that may be used by classes of avatar other than the crafter, thus connecting the classes socially through the various equipment their specializations require.

A Wide Range of Alternatives

Many MMOs do not require selecting a specific small set of crafting professions, but follow different philosophies of specialization. In *Anarchy Online*, progress up the fully 220 levels of general experience earns improvement points, which may be invested as the player wishes.[5] The standard summary states:

> Your skills define what you can do, and how good you are at it. Items have skill requirements for using and or equipping them, nano programs have requirements for uploading and executing them. At each level, your character is awarded a certain amount of Improvement Points. These allow you to raise the skills that in turn allow you to use better weapons, armour, nano-programs and other general equipment. It is not possible to maximise all the skills, as you are not awarded enough IPs to do so; therefore you have to concentrate on the areas of most use to your character...[6]

AO takes place on a planet named Rubi-Ka, and a very extensive online database called People of Rubi-Ka offers quantitative data, but does not include information about avatars' improvement point distributions.[7]

---

[5] Bainbridge, W.S. *Computer Simulations of Space Societies*, 223–30. Cham, Switzerland: Springer.

[6] www.ao-universe.com/index.php?id=14&site=AO-Universe%2FKnowledge% 2F&pid=402&lang=en

[7] people.anarchy-online.com

However, to understand how crafting skills fit into the larger social structure, we can use as a proxy variable the general avatar class, confusingly called *professions* in *Anarchy Online*, as suggested in an online article titled Introduction to Tradeskilling:

> Some professions are "made" for tradeskilling, by this I mean that they have a lot of items that can be used to increase tradeskill skills, they have good bonuses in armour that is specific for them and to spend Improvement Points on tradeskills isn't as costly as for professions that are not "made" for Tradeskilling. The professions that have a good toolset when it comes to tradeskilling in particular are Engineers and Traders. However there are quite a few professions that have a particular tradeskill they are good with. For example, Meta-Physicists and Nanotechnicians with their Nano Programming, Fixers with Break and Entry skill, Doctors with PhamaTech.[8]

In *Anarchy Online*, guilds are often called *organizations*, and the designers require creation of one to involve six players who decide which of six size-structures to adopt, five of them requiring one player to be the formal leader:

> Department: seven ranks (president, general, squad commander, unit commander, unit leader, unit member, applicant)
> Republic: five ranks (president, advisor, veteran, member, applicant)
> Faction: five ranks (director, board member, executive, member, applicant)
> Feudalism: four ranks (lord, knight, vassal, peasant)
> Monarchy: three ranks (monarch, counsel, follower)
> Anarchism: one rank (anarchist)

All except anarchism, in which decisions are supposed to be made by majority vote, are highly stratified. New members automatically go into the lowest rank and can be raised to a higher rank only by members

---

[8] www.ao-universe.com/index.php?id=14&site=AO-Universe%2FKnowledge%2F&mid=&pid=387

who already are higher. The practical implication of rank in most organizations is unclear or minimal, and much of the activity on the planet Rubi-Ka can be completed solo. Therefore, it may be that avatars are promoted only if they frequently participate in team combat missions, and many of the lowest-rank members are respected for other functions they perform, such as manufacturing. They cannot avoid combat altogether, because they need it to earn improvement points to invest in tradeskills, but exploring vast Rubi-Ka and doing solo missions are quite sufficient for that. For the present analysis, I focused on organizations structured as departments, not merely having selected that choice at founding but actually having promoted some members, finding 205 organizations with at least 100 members each, at least 20 of which were above applicant rank. Each organization had its own page of data listing all the members, which could be manually scraped and pasted into a spreadsheet, which ultimately had 136,259 rows of data, 1 for each avatar. Table 5.3 shows their distribution across the seven status ranks, including columns for four of the professions most suitable for tradeskilling.

Even among the 205 organizations that did promote at least 20 of their members, most were never promoted, 100,674 out of 136,259. The mean experience level among applicants is the lowest of any rank, 105 out of the 220 maximum, but reaching level 105 takes a lot of time and effort. The status ranks would not graph perfectly as a pyramid, given that squad commanders outnumber those in each of the three unit ranks, and I tend to think that we are really seeing three overlaid structures. The presidents, generals, and squad commanders represent a combat core membership of the organization. The unit ranks represent a combat periphery, with some of the avatars being alts of main avatars that have higher ranks. The applicants represent more casual or solo players, and many who played the game for a while and then quit, without being rejected from the corporation but possibly reduced in rank. This structure resembles the social structures reported in many studies of open-source software communities, which distinguish core from peripheral participants, often implying a wider population of interested but relatively inactive members outside the so-called periphery.[9]

---

[9] Lee, G.K., and R.E. Cole. 2003. "From a Firm-Based to a Community-Based Model of Knowledge Creation: The Case of the Linux Kernel Development."

Table 5.3 Fractions of organization ranks in each of four commercial classes

Rank	Mean level	Total number	Percent engineers	Percent traders	Percent nano-technicians	Percent doctors
President	205	220	8.2%	4.5%	5.5%	10.0%
General	181	3,338	7.8%	6.1%	5.2%	11.3%
Squad commander	166	13,266	7.1%	6.4%	6.3%	9.4%
Unit commander	133	4,494	7.4%	6.7%	8.5%	8.4%
Unit leader	129	2,292	7.2%	6.8%	8.0%	6.9%
Unit member	131	11,975	7.8%	7.4%	7.6%	8.0%
Applicant	105	100,674	7.4%	6.9%	7.9%	8.1%
Total	117	136,259	7.4%	6.9%	7.7%	8.3%

Engineers appear equally distributed across the 7 membership ranks, keeping in mind the small number of generals and thus the imprecision of its 8.2 percent figure. Traders and nano-technicians seem less common at higher ranks, whereas doctors are more common. This may reflect the fact that doctors' healing function may be needed directly in combat, whereas the other two professions may produce valuables outside of combat. But given that profession is only a proxy for tradeskill, and some of the percentage differences are small, we cannot have great confidence about how informative this analysis is about manufacture in *Anarchy Online*. More reasonably, it suggests that many questions need to be asked, especially in observational studies of real-world distributed manufacturing, about how technical skills will factor into social status.

RuneScape is an example of an MMO in which all players are allowed to develop all the specialty skills, of which there are 27, several of which relate to manufacture. At the present time, players enter either free-to-play, which gives them only 17 of these skills, whereas paying subscribers can advance skill in all 27.[10] Most begin at experience level 1 and can be advanced through practice to level 99. One exception is constitution, which begins at level 10 and is not conceptualized as a skill in other MMOs but as a fundamental characteristic of the avatar's general experience level. A wiki explains:

> Constitution (also known as health, and formerly as Hitpoints or HP) is a combat skill that affects how many life points (LP) a player or monster has. Life points represent the amount of damage a player or monster can withstand before it dies. Death occurs when a player or monster's life points reach zero. The current minimum requirement to be ranked (at approximately rank 1,500,945) on the hi-scores for Constitution is level 15. As of

Organization Science 14, pp. 633–49; Crowston, K., and I. Shamshurin. 2016. "Core-Periphery Communication and the Success of Free/Libre Open Source Software Projects." In *Proceedings of the IFIP International Conference on Open Source Systems*, 45–56. Springer.

[10] runescape.wikia.com/wiki/Skills

16 August 2018, there are 240,048 current members that have achieved level 99 in Constitution.[11]

Current data on avatar achievement can be obtained from a website that offers a vast amount of detailed information, much of it organized as leaderboards.[12] Table 5.4 offers data collected on September 30, 2018, on over a million *RuneScape* avatars, expressed as a summary of the leaderboards, thus representing the status distribution for each of the skills, which begin with constitution, followed by a dozen production-related skills. The minimum skill level reported is 15, so beginning players are excluded. The online database can be set to report all the avatars in descending order of a particular skill, and 1,535,488 had reached level 15 in constitution already, 34,543 more than the wiki editor had found back on August 16. It was straightforward to jump quickly down the list of avatars to find the one ranked exactly 250,000, and that one was at constitution skill 98, whereas the one at rank 500,000 was at skill 80.

All avatars have the constitution skill, but in principle the others in Table 5.4 are optional, although the ones that immediately follow it are trained in the tutorial. Among the first tasks performed by a new avatar is chopping wood, making a fire, and cooking over it. Mining is trained immediately afterward. The first craft in which fewer than a million avatars are counted as having reached level 15 is fletching, which frankly is somewhat specialized, as the skills page of the wiki explains: "Create projectiles (such as arrows, bolts, and darts) and bows/crossbows."[13] The four even less popular skills in Table 5.4 are those that require a paid subscription, also described on that page:

Construction: Allows players to build a house and its contents, such as chairs, tables, workshops, dungeons, and more. Every player's house is located inside its own instance, separated from the rest of the game. Portals around the world are used to gain entry into the player's own house, and to gain access to other

[11] runescape.wikia.com/wiki/Constitution

[12] services.runescape.com/m=clan-hiscores/c=TN64L9O2kLw/ranking

[13] runescape.wikia.com/wiki/Skills

Table 5.4 *Avatar level comparison across economically significant skills*

Selected avatar skills	Avatars at skill 15 or above	Skill level of the avatar at rank						
		250,000	500,000	750,000	1,000,000	1,250,000	1,500,000
Constitution	1,535,488	98	80	64	48	30	15
Woodcutting	1,306,507	90	76	61	43	20	
Mining	1,247,867	80	65	52	36		
Cooking	1,229,481	90	70	54	37		
Firemaking	1,217,412	90	70	53	35		
Smithing	1,173,075	82	63	48	33		
Fishing	1,150,083	85	68	54	33		
Crafting	1,081,080	81	61	46	26		
Fletching	900,161	87	67	37			
Construction	750,865	76	48	15			
Hunting	715,336	74	49				
Farming	680,787	71	38				
Invention	213,323						

players' houses, allowing anyone to gain access to some of the very useful, high level rooms and furniture.

Hunting: Allows players to track, net, deadfall, snare, and trap animals for their hides, abilities and treasures. Some of the animals caught can be used in other skills.

Farming: Allows players to grow plants (such as fruits, vegetables, herbs, or trees) in certain patches across the world of RuneScape. Farming is notably very useful for collecting many common and rare herbs for Herblore.

Invention: Allows players to disassemble many in game items in order to break them down into components used in creating new contraptions. These contraptions can benefit the player in a number of ways, including upgrading and increasing the damage of a weapon.

Anarchy Online and *RuneScape* show that the division of labor in manufacturing-oriented social systems can still vary even when tradeskills are not limited to two or three as in *World of Warcraft* and *Lord of the Rings Online*. In principle, avatars in *Anarchy Online* could learn all the crafting skills, but the need to invest improvement points from a limited supply prevents them from doing so. In *RuneScape*, learning more skills costs time and effort, but any sufficiently motivated player can simultaneously climb all the status ladders. In real-world small-scale distributed manufacturing, the nature of the product and the processes required to make it may determine whether workers must master a small number of skillsets, as in *World of Warcraft* and *Lord of the Rings Online*, or can develop unique patterns of skills covering a wider range, as in *Anarchy Online* and *RuneScape*.

The Most Classic of the Virtual Worlds

The oldest MMO examined in this study is *Ultima Online*, still very much alive after more than two decades. Although, like other successful role-playing games, UO required a good deal of combat, the emphasis was really on assembling teams of players, collecting simulated natural resources, and constructing homes and fortresses. Thus, it fulfills the definition of *virtual world* and is capable of being a location for socio-logical field research. Other sources of information include several online wikis and encyclopedias, plus text-based discussion forums. Among several other UO forums, Stratics proclaims itself "the oldest continually running MMORPG Fansite on the Internet," providing vast information to the UO community since 1997.[14] Like WoW and LotRO, UO exists in several distinct Internet server versions—*shards* or *instances*—the same world but serving different populations of players. The section of the forum devoted to shard-specific communications contained 10,675 forum discussions containing 48,431 messages, for the Atlantic shard I had studied via participant observation.

Rather than focus on the forums, to get a sense of the social structure of the Atlantic shard I myself had explored required searching for its guilds on UA's official website.[15] The database is rather complex, and much manual labor was required to transfer the data into a spreadsheet for analysis. One selects a shard and then must enter a name, in either a character (avatar) or guild search field, and I could have begun by collecting the names of avatars who posted in real time on the Atlantic text chat. To explore methodological options, I tried other approaches. I searched online for names of prominent guilds, finding a couple of lists, and discovered other guilds by entering search terms likely to be the first word of many guild names, such as *clan*, *empire*, and *lord*. I found other guilds by searching for avatars having very common first names, finding 509 of whom exactly 200 belonged to 96 guilds. Many guilds were inactive, notably Lords of Chaos which listed 51 members, but not a single one had been active in the previous 90 days, so no data about them were available.

Finding a guild in the database allowed one to see a full list of all its active members, each name being a link to a page giving a few statistics describing the particular avatar. Concentrating just on guilds having at least 25 members, I wound up with the data shown in Table 5.5, for 24 guilds and 3,398 active avatars in 2017. If one were funded to perform a major research project, it might be possible to write software to scrape all

---

[14] stratics.com

[15] uo.com/myuo-2/#/search

Table 5.5 Census of two dozen guilds in the Atlantic shard of Ultima Online

| Guild | Avatar members | Percent who are | | Mean skill-related statistics | | | |
		Elves	Female	Strength	Dexterity	Intelligence
United We Fight	899	47.1%	32.7%	109.8	55.2	75.9
HOT	509	44.4%	38.1%	113.7	56.4	82.1
The Syndicate	500	41.2%	33.8%	107.9	55.4	79.8
The Wheel of Time	209	42.1%	40.7%	109.3	55.1	77.1
Fated to Win	120	25.0%	33.3%	111.9	60.1	81.0
99 Bottles	117	32.5%	29.1%	96.9	46.4	75.3
Dread Pirates of Sosaria	95	46.3%	18.9%	106.0	54.1	75.5
House of Skye	79	3.8%	87.3%	47.5	24.7	84.2
Helping Hands Young Club	73	46.6%	38.4%	96.3	43.9	83.5
Owned on Another Shard	71	40.8%	31.0%	113.9	60.0	84.0
Kitty Kat Club	70	38.6%	58.6%	97.5	49.3	62.1
We Are Everywhere	68	52.9%	0.0%	41.5	18.9	57.5
Euro Stars	63	46.0%	36.5%	111.7	71.4	70.4
Rhonai	61	3.3%	45.9%	59.0	22.6	28.8
Death Riders	60	43.3%	65.0%	93.9	52.4	72.2

Blood Order of Brotherhood	59	23.7%	35.6%	112.6	46.8	84.1
The Brotherhood of the Dragon	58	46.6%	37.9%	110.2	45.3	76.3
Defenders of the Peace	54	33.3%	46.3%	107.5	54.5	72.2
Survivors of the Storm	44	29.5%	40.9%	109.5	51.8	76.5
Empire of Oceania Blade	42	11.9%	78.6%	46.2	30.6	53.1
Four Horsemen	41	51.2%	41.5%	105.6	43.7	86.4
Clan of Khaos	38	39.5%	52.6%	97.1	49.9	84.1
The Gray Corps	36	0.0%	19.4%	71.8	26.7	58.3
Leather Neck Raiders	32	25.0%	25.0%	107.1	43.4	88.9

the data off the web automatically, but in this case all the work was manual, a mixture of typing and copy–paste actions, taking almost exactly 1 minute per avatar, or about 7 full 8-hour work days, not counting the many hours invested in participant observation and working out the data collection method. In creating an avatar, a player must select its gender and race, there being three races: Human, Elf, and the rare Gargoyles.

For each avatar, it was possible to copy several pieces of information about its skill set, which effectively defined the particular avatar's typical role in the social division of labor of long-term guilds and brief adventure teams.[16] Fundamental are three characteristics called *strength*, *dexterity*, and *intelligence*. Players often call them *stats*, short for *statistics*. An avatar gains points in these variables by taking a vast number of specialized actions inside the virtual world. Each skill-related statistic has a maximum of 125, and the total of all three cannot exceed 260, thus enforcing a division of labor in which avatars must specialize. The highest average total of 257.9 belongs to the 71-avatar guild, Owned on Another Shard, whose name suggests it belongs to very dedicated players who are active on multiple UA shards. Fully 46 of its 71 avatars have reached the very difficult goal of 260 primary stat points. Dedicated players may have multiple avatars, but getting them to the top skill levels may take hundreds of hours. Avatars can be conceptualized as roles, as positions in a social organization, or in other sociological terms. That requires understanding the values of the stats, suggested by their formal definitions:

Strength—Determines how much can be carried, amount of melee damage, and number of hit points

Dexterity—Determines stamina and is important for skills such as snooping and parrying

Intelligence—Determines the amount of mana a player has and can affect skills such as magery[17]

Hit points, also called *health* in many other virtual worlds and *morale* in *Lord of the Rings Online*, refer to the variable that determines when the

---

[16] uo.com/wiki/ultima-online-wiki/player/stats/skills-stats-and-attributes

[17] www.uoguide.com/Stats

avatar will lose a fight, which happens if hit points are beaten down by an enemy to zero. Hit points tend to regenerate, can be increased temporarily by various actions, and are seldom meaningful outside of combat. So, avatars that primarily play combat roles will tend to increase their strength to the maximum, which means that one or both of the other two stats must be weaker. But strength is also important for *crafting* useful virtual objects and architecture, because that work requires carrying heavy things. *Mana* is like hit points, but measures the momentary reserve of magical power the avatar possesses. Therefore, intelligence is valued by avatars with magical roles, such as healing comrades during combat or performing alchemy to produce healing or empowering potions that can be used at a later time. Strength, dexterity, and intelligence can be considered primary statistics of an avatar, whereas healing and alchemy abilities are secondary statistics in a set of dozens, and the dataset includes information about both categories.[18] Table 5.5 shows quite clearly that the guilds differ not only in their level and distributions of average stats, but also in the fractions of avatars that are Elves or females.

A total of 56 different skills were among the three most developed for at least one of the 3,398 avatars in Table 5.5, the most popular being magery, the ability to cast magic spells, placed with the other most popular skills in the middle of Table 5.6 which prioritizes crafting skills. In second place and possessed by 901 avatars was "evaluating intelligence," a skill that increases the damage of offensive spells, and 599 were skilled at meditation which increases the supply of mana required for spell casting.[19] Often, avatars would combine this trio. The fact that the three most popular specialized skills all concerned magic-based battle highlights the fantasy orientation of *Ultima Online*, and in fourth place with 582 avatars was resisting spells. Most other popular skills concern nonmagical combat, except for animal lore and animal taming, which allowed avatars to take charge of wild animal NPCs. Table 5.6 shows that manufacturing skills were much less popular, indicating that a relatively small subset of avatars produced goods to give or sell to warriors, in this virtual world's division of labor.

---

[18] wiki.ultimacodex.com/wiki/Ultima_Online_Skills
[19] wiki.ultimacodex.com/wiki/Magery

Table 5.6 Popularity of crafting skills and the related statistics in Ultima Online

Crafting skills	Number of Avatars	Mean Skill-Related Statistics			
		Strength	Dexterity	Intelligence	Total
Blacksmithy	250	107.1	38.8	65.3	211.2
Tailoring	214	111.7	41.3	68.5	221.5
Arms lore	86	110.3	42.5	64.4	217.2
Alchemy	85	99.0	36.3	79.9	215.2
Fishing	76	104.6	46.4	74.3	225.3
Cartography	68	106.9	29.0	96.7	232.6
Mining	62	101.5	39.4	59.6	200.5
Bowcraft and fletching	53	92.7	40.3	63.1	196.1
Carpentry	45	110.0	44.5	63.8	218.3
Tinkering	42	95.1	27.1	61.1	183.3
Lumberjacking	31	100.5	51.5	47.0	199.0
Cooking	30	89.2	37.5	75.0	201.7

More popular skills					
Magery	1,024	101.1	23.5	104.1	228.7
Evaluating intelligence	901	100.9	23.8	106.7	231.4
Meditation	599	91.1	25.0	98.0	214.1
Resisting spells	582	109.0	61.1	77.7	247.8
Anatomy	579	106.7	101.8	34.9	243.4
Tactics	574	106.5	101.4	33.4	241.3
Animal lore	565	111.6	25.7	106.3	243.6
Focus	469	80.3	35.6	76.4	192.3
Archery	328	104.6	100.8	38.5	243.9
Parry	308	109.7	93.6	42.1	245.4
Animal taming	292	110.0	26.2	102.2	238.4

The user interface for *Ultima Online* gives players the option to set a control determining whether a statistic will stay at its current level, increase if additional points become available, or decrease as some other skill increases. Thus, players can gradually change their specialization through a combination of setting controls and doing work. As with stats, skills have a combined maximum, which is 720 rather than 260. Interface controls select which skills should be increased by practice.[20] There also exist many NPC skill trainers and other aspects to the skill development system. It is not obvious how these complexities may model further realities in distributed manufacturing, but there may be an analogy to the formal process of gaining accreditation or licensing to practice a skill. Governments and professional societies will need to develop new norms for the technical occupations of the future, especially if artificial intelligence and other innovations render work more part-time or combine subspecialties in dynamic ways.

Skill Structures Within Voluntary Organizations

The fact that MMOs differ greatly in the kinds and structures of data publicly available presents not only challenges for researchers, but also opportunities. This section will examine the very different leaderboards of *Black Desert Online* and *Dark Age of Camelot*, to get a sense of this variety. Wikipedia says *Black Desert Online* is "a sandbox-oriented massively multiplayer online role-playing game by Korean video game developer Pearl Abyss" that "takes place in a high fantasy setting and revolves around the conflict between two rival nations, the Republic of Calpheon and the Kingdom of Valencia. Calpheon is very materialistic whereas Valencia is very spiritual."[21]

One of the Pearl Abyss websites notes the complex social structure that exists around this virtual world, listing seven different publishers who managed this MMO and its servers in different parts of the world: Kakao Games (Korea, North America, part of Europe, Oceania), GameOn (Japan), GameNet (Russia), Pearl Abyss Taiwan (Taiwan), Red Fox

---

[20] www.uoguide.com/Skills
[21] en.wikipedia.org/wiki/Black_Desert_Online

Games (South America), Pearl Abyss MEA (Turkey and MEA [Middle East Asia]), and Pearl Abyss SEA (Thai and SEA [South East Asia]).[22] However, Wikipedia also notes the instability of some of these corporate relationships:

> In October 2015, Black Desert Online was published and localized in Russia by Cypriot publisher GameNet. This contract expired on October 12, 2018 without an agreement as to account information, including character data. Pearl Abyss has apologized to Russian players and announced they would self-publish in Russia when their own localization efforts were completed.

Again, we can conceptualize the game companies as simulations of the information technology companies that will support distributed manufacturing through licensing software and supporting data archives. Although GameNet is usually called a publisher, it apparently was responsible for localization, which basically means translating all the text of the software and game story into Russian, and it also managed the Internet servers. Thus, GameNet held all the data about the players' avatars, most importantly their current status in *Black Desert Online*, the virtual goods and money the avatars possessed, and even their social relationships represented by friendship ties to other avatars and guild memberships. The generally reliable Massively Overpowered news blogsite reported in September 2018 that negotiations had not been completed between GameNet and Pearl Abyss, and for several weeks it seemed possible that all the player data would be lost and Pearl Abyss would need to create a Russian version of Black Desert Online from scratch.[23]

I explored the North American version of *Black Desert Online* in the spring of 2018, focusing on crafting. Although the high levels of the game emphasize PvP conflict, at low and medium levels there are relatively safe territories. Whereas *World of Warcraft* had three quite separate harvesting

---

[22] www.pearlabyss.com/games/BDO?lang=en
[23] Royce, B. 2018. "Black Desert's Russian Servers will be Spared from Their Abrupt and Messy Closure after All." *Massively Overpowered*, October 17. massivelyop.com/2018/10/17/black-desert-russian-fiasco-unfiascoed/

professions—herbalism, mining, and skinning—Black Desert Online combines them with several others in a single *gathering* profession, requiring different tools for each form of harvesting. For example, an axe is required to chop wood from trees, and a pickaxe to extract minerals from mining nodes. WoW's skinning profession becomes two aspects of gathering in BDO, using a tanning knife to take fur from an animal that has been killed or a butchering knife to get its meat.[24]

Inside the game, an information display can be accessed that includes leaderboards for guilds, giving the names and point scores of groups rather than individual avatars. On May 5, 2018, I took screenshots of the rankings of 573 guilds on the 4 harvesting and 4 crafting skills, then manually copied the data into a spreadsheet for analysis. For each skill the top 400 guilds were listed, and forum discussions of players seem to agree that the rankings are based directly upon the total number of skill points the members had achieved.[25] Data of this kind in this form pose problems for researchers, and we would prefer the actual point scores for all the guilds, not just those in the top 400 for each of the variables. An obvious issue is that if the ranks are point score totals they reflect the variable sizes of the guilds, which range from 20 to 100 with a mean of 62 members. Table 5.7 lists the correlations between the 4 harvesting skills and all 8 of the manufacturing-related skills, plus the 8 correlations with the size of the guild membership, which average –0.67, a negative correlation because the top guilds have low ranks. The population bias is illustrated by the fact that 2 guilds are ranked 1 for 3 of the skills each; 1 other is ranked 1 for 2 skills, and their memberships are 97, 98, and 100. The coefficients in the table are Pearson's *r*, which can converge on Spearman's *rho* when rank scores do not contain duplicates, but a technically more sophisticated analysis would attempt to control for the factor of guild membership, although that might not be easy.

The correlations are all very high, which undoubtedly reflects the contaminating effect of guild size. The one obvious finding is that hunting has lower correlations, both with the other harvesting or crafting skills and with guild size. To be sure, it is impossible to explore this virtual

---

[24] blackdesertonline.wikia.com/wiki/Gathering
[25] www.reddit.com/r/blackdesertonline/comments/4hrn4l/guild_ranking/

Table 5.7 Correlations between guild rankings for harvesting and crafting skills

	Gathering	Fishing	Hunting	Farming	Members
Gathering	1.00	0.92	0.75	0.85	-0.70
Fishing	0.92	1.00	0.73	0.81	-0.75
Hunting	0.75	0.73	1.00	0.71	-0.57
Farming	0.85	0.81	0.71	1.00	-0.66
Cooking	0.93	0.92	0.72	0.79	-0.69
Alchemy	0.89	0.84	0.72	0.83	-0.62
Processing	0.94	0.93	0.70	0.81	-0.67
Trade	0.93	0.95	0.72	0.83	-0.69

world without killing many beasts, but hunting is more specialized, as a player-authored guide reports:

> Hunting has always been the odd child out of the Life Skills. Many people trash the skill and avoid it in general, but few ever stop to question "maybe it's just misunderstood?" Hunting is about finding creatures that can't be killed with regular weapons and shooting them with a gun. If nothing else hunting is a fun activity, but it also rewards the player with materials and rare ingredients.[26]

Thus the lower correlations for hunting do not reflect the fact that all avatars need to kill animals, but rather that special effort invested in certain locations is required, rendered somewhat uninteresting because of all the other killing of simulated animals all players must experience.

The system of *Black Desert Online* leaderboards is interesting for the way it rewards groups for the accomplishments of their members, rather than assigning status only to individual avatars. But because decisions about investing in harvesting and crafting are chiefly made by individuals, this means that statistical research on the relationships between these activities is not very productive. The situation in *Dark Age of Camelot* is very different. MMORPG.com classifies both BDO and DAoC as fantasy games, but I prefer to classify *Dark Age of Camelot* as historical, because it is set in the European Dark Ages and includes representations of several real locations I have studied in the field, notably Stonehenge and the Roman Wall in Britain. Two versions of DAoC exist, represented by different servers or server clusters. The Gaheris server minimizes conflict between players, emphasizing missions to explore this simulation of ancient history and allowing all avatars to communicate and cooperate. Most players operate on the Ywain cluster, which organizes PvP combat on a very large scale, involving sieges of castles as well as small battles in the field. DAoC's main website explains the system thus:

> There are three distinct Realms in Dark Age of Camelot—Albion, Midgard and Hibernia. Think of these three Realms as foreign

---

[26] grumpygreen.cricket/bdo-hunting-guide-eminent.html

countries with well defended borders and different languages. An integral part of Dark Age of Camelot is the concept of Realms. Realms are entirely independent worlds that exist within the larger world of the game. Although there are some exceptions to this, the primary principle is that each of the Realms is at war with each of the others, and that they cannot even communicate with each other. Realm vs. Realm combat (known as RvR) occurs in special level-specific battlegrounds and in the New Frontiers. There are battlegrounds available for characters level 1 to 49. Battlegrounds are smaller RvR areas and entry into each is limited by level. The first battleground is level 1–4, the next is 5–9, the third is 10–14, and so forth, ending at level 49. The battlegrounds are a good place to learn how to use your RvR skills before venturing out into the main RvR zones in New Frontiers.[27]

While set in days or yore, *Dark Age of Camelot* is a marvelous simulation of large-scale social interaction, much of it involving preparation for war through training of individual skills and manufacture of equipment, even of large siege machinery. Over a period of weeks ending in mid-October 2018, I collected data from the extensive dataset of avatars available from Camelot Herald, in which one page of information exists for every avatar, including what guild it may belong to.[28] *Black Desert Online* may limit the membership of each guild to 100 avatars because that encourages development of cohesive social groups in which a significant fraction of the members may be important. *Dark Age of Camelot* does not set such low limits, and one guild I found had 5,033 avatars belonging to 1,530 player accounts. As many as 21 guilds can form an alliance, sharing access to their many facilities, including guild halls.[29] I searched for comparable alliances across the three factions in the Ywain server complex, finding one in the Albion faction to which 15,342 avatars belonged, one in Hibernia with 13,047 avatars, and one in Midgard with 14,886. Each guild had a home page in Camelot Herald from which its

---

[27] darkageofcamelot.com/content/rvr-server-types

[28] search.camelotherald.com/#/search

[29] camelotherald.wikia.com/wiki/Create_a_Guild_House

full membership list could be accessed, but it also had a leaderboard listing the top 10 members in 6 manufacturing skills. Table 5.8 summarizes
the tradeskill levels of the 1,882 high-status avatars listed in all the leaderboards, 603 in Albion, 630 in Hibernia, and 649 in Midgard.

Siegecraft did not have a leaderboard, but it was easy to copy the
statistic in this manufacturing craft for any avatar listed as superior in
any of the six leaderboards. The total number of guilds was 62, so we
might expect the total number of avatars in Table 5.8 to be 62 × 6 ×
10 = 3,720, rather than the 1,882 that were found, but in fact some
ambitious players had achieved high leaderboard status in more than one
tradeskill, and some of the smallest guilds lack avatars that were skilled
in some fields. Another comparison worth noting is that only 1,882 of
a total 43,275, or 4.3 percent, had reached high status in any of the 6
leaderboard tradeskills, whereas those 1,882 had done so in an average of
about 2 of these manufacturing skills. This demonstrates that each manufacturing category was a rare specialization, just as we might expect them
to be in the real communities of the future that incorporate significant
local manufacturing.

The correlation coefficients in Table 5.8 look much more reasonable
than those in Table 5.7, rather like those we get with opinion items in
public polls. The four tradeskills chosen to define columns of the table
were those that most efficiently illustrated the structure of the entire correlation matrix. Here is how the pages in the *Dark Age of Camelot* wiki
describe all seven tradeskills:

> Spellcrafting gives players the ability to craft magical gems that imbue
> their armor and weapons with enhancements to various skills and
> attributes suited to one's character.[30]
> Alchemy gives players the ability to craft potions, poisons, dyes, and
> tinctures. Poisons are primarily used by the assassin classes (Infiltra-
> tor, Shadowblade, and Nightshade) for dealing extra damage and
> negative effects on their targets. Potions are basically a bottled spell,
> which will cast itself upon the user when consumed. Dyes can be

---

[30] camelotherald.wikia.com/wiki/Spellcrafting

Table 5.8 *Tradeskills in the Ywain simulation of Dark Ages of western Europe*

Manufacturing skill	Skill level achieved		Correlation				
	Maximum	Mean	Alchemy	Armorcraft	Fletching	Siegecraft
Spellcrafting	1,104	353	0.39	0.17	0.01	0.12
Alchemy	1,151	390	1.00	0.12	0.03	0.20
Armorcraft	1,167	350	0.12	1.00	0.25	0.26
Fletching	1,150	210	0.03	0.25	1.00	0.27
Tailoring	1,167	332	0.10	0.35	0.30	0.19
Weaponcraft	1,150	307	0.15	0.38	0.28	0.28
Siegecraft	1,050	200	0.20	0.26	0.27	1.00

used on armors, shields, and cloaks to change their color. Tinctures are used to place special spells on other crafted items, in the form of charges, procs, and reactive procs.[31]

Armorcrafting is the tradeskill that uses the strongest materials available to produce heavier armors, such as chain or plate. An Armorcrafter's final product may be magically enhanced through Spellcrafting.[32]

Fletching focuses on the creation of bows, staves, and musical instruments. The archer classes (Scout, Hunter, and Ranger) may find this craft the most useful as they can craft bows to use as their ranged weapon of choice.[33]

Tailoring produces lighter types of armor, such as Cloth and Leather. Tailors use various cloths and leathers to craft armor for casters, rogues, and other light tank classes. Much like Armorcrafting, the products of a Tailor may also be spellcrafted to become many times more powerful.[34]

Weaponcrafting focuses on creating powerful weapons such as swords and spears. The weapons created by Weaponcrafters may also be spellcrafted to become more powerful.[35]

Siegecrafting was completely revamped and fleshed out into a full tradeskill in version 1.90. Recipes now range from 5 to 1000 skill, covering everything from weak, makeshift devices to fully fortified engines of war.[36]

It would be simplistic to say that spellcrafting and alchemy correlate more strongly with each other, at 0.39, because they are both "magical." Actually, the fantasy quality of this historical simulation adds a legendary quality to the story, but these tradeskills are comparable to the manufacture of mechanical or electronic accessories, and chemicals, that enhance the performance of other technologies. Spellcrafting is actually highly

[31] camelotherald.wikia.com/wiki/Alchemy
[32] camelotherald.wikia.com/wiki/Armorcraft
[33] camelotherald.wikia.com/wiki/Fletching
[34] camelotherald.wikia.com/wiki/Tailoring
[35] camelotherald.wikia.com/wiki/Weaponcraft
[36] camelotherald.wikia.com/wiki/Siegecraft

technical, and its most serious practitioners use Kort's Spellcrafting Calculator, a program that allows the user to figure the best alternatives for producing an enhancer for a particular weapon or piece of armor.[37] The descriptions for alchemy and fletching specify which classes of avatars can best use their products, and of course classes differ in whether they use protective equipment made from metal (armorcrafting) or cloth and leather (tailoring). The descriptions for armorcrafting, tailoring, and weaponcrafting mention that their products can be enhanced by spellcrafting. This is not true for fletching which has a zero correlation with spellcrafting.

Of course, one reason why an avatar may develop two particular tradeskills is that they may use similar raw materials, such as armorcrafting and weaponcrafting that both use metal and correlate at 0.38. At low levels, raw materials may be purchased from merchants, but at high levels some must be gathered or looted during adventures. Also, some crafts share manufacturing equipment. For example, both spellcrafters and alchemists use an alchemy table. The tradeskill system has gone through several changes during the long history of *Dark Age of Camelot*, and prior to 2008 each craft was restricted to certain adventure classes.[38] Siegecrafting was added and altered, notably in 2007 when an update announced: "No longer are unrelated tradeskills required to build these machines. All siege ingredient and apparatus recipes have been moved from the original, primary tradeskills into Siegecrafting."[39]

Conclusion

A general question in the sociology of social structures is the extent to which relationships are between living people or functional roles. In the virtual worlds considered here, each person may be represented by multiple avatars, and in a *Dark Age of Camelot* guild with 1,530 players, each one had roughly 3.3 avatars, not counting any they may have had in other guilds, factions, or games. Players tend to use the word *avatar* when the

---

[37] kscraft.sourceforge.net/

[38] camelot.allakhazam.com/db/skills.html?cskill=176

[39] camelotherald.wikia.com/wiki/Patch_Notes:_Version_1.90

virtual being represents themselves personally, or *character* when it represents a prescripted role, so they are quite conscious of that sociological distinction. They are also quite aware that the large-scale social structures contain artificial people as well, such as the simulation of the real deceased scholar, Snorri Sturluson, who stands at the gate to Jordheim, the capital city of Midgard. The term NPC or non-player character is commonly used, but in the case of virtual Sturluson we could coin the new term, *non-player avatar*, given that it represents a real if deceased person. Without going that deep into philosophy, we should consider the roles played in social structures by simulated people.

CHAPTER 6

Artificial Intelligence in the Human–Technology System

The most obvious form of artificial intelligence (AI) in MMOs is the large population of non-player characters (NPCs), some of which simply provide information, or are economic vendors, or assign predefined missions. But a few which interact physically, as in the case of combat enemies, may exhibit real AI through their movements and reactions to the actions of the player's avatar. Although some have a little local autonomy, most NPCs are really just interface points to the massive database that supports the world. Especially worthy of examination are those called *pets* or *companions*, essentially *secondary avatars* that help the player's main avatar. In addition to giving them commands, the user can train them; they can learn to some extent through their own experience, and they can take on distinctive identities, seeming almost like a real friend of the person.

It seems likely that the computer-controlled local manufacturing equipment of the future will possess features that could be called *artificial intelligence*, for example, a milling device that automatically works out the exact sequence of cutting required to shape a piece of wood to fit the customer's design. But two other related forms of AI may also become common: (1) personalized communication with the user by means of simulated people like Apple's virtual assistant Siri[1] and (2) less obvious distributed intelligence operating across a wide system of technologies and information resources.[2] It may be worth distinguishing *AI* from

---

[1] en.wikipedia.org/wiki/Siri

[2] Bainbridge, W.S., E.E. Brent, K.M. Carley, D.R. Heise, M.W. Macy, B. Markovsky, and J. Skvoretz. 1994. "Artificial Social Intelligence." *Annual Review of Sociology* 20, pp. 407–36.

simulated intelligence, AI being explicit representation of cognitive processes and SI following more implicit design principles, pretending to be intelligent in order to strengthen the significance for real human beings.

Primitive but Complex Artificial Intelligence

The simplest form of a real AI is a rudimentary "neural net" consisting of memory registers containing numbers that represent the probability that the simulated person would perform this preprogrammed action versus that one.[3] For example, many MMOs have the option to set a companion to fight an enemy that attacked the player's avatar, but switch over to healing the main avatar if it becomes seriously damaged. In *Star Trek Online*, not only does each NPC crewmember develop specific abilities, but the user can in real time switch on and off various options, different ones for different companions in a team of four. Here the emphasis will be on the roles played by avatars in the manufacturing system, including the main avatar as well as the secondaries. Yet, given the emphasis in the games themselves on combat, we can fully understand the nature of avatar AI only in the wider context.

A very recent if ethically crude example is the virtual slaves called *thralls* in *Conan Exiles*.[4] Rather dramatically, thralls are NPCs of many types, which the main avatar can club unconscious in the wild, drag back to the avatar's home base, and train to be obedient by making them labor to exhaustion in a wheel of pain "that strengthens the body as it breaks the mind."[5] Some thralls are designed to operate manufacturing equipment as substitutes for the avatar and thus for the player. A great variety of other games conceptualize simulated assistants of the human user more humanely and portray a process of mutual learning between them.

---

[3] Bainbridge, W.S. 1987. *Sociology Laboratory*. Belmont, California: Wadsworth. 1995. "Minimum Intelligent Neural Device: A Tool for Social Simulation." Mathematical Sociology 20, pp. 179–92; 1995. "Neural Network Models of Religious Belief." Sociological Perspectives 38, pp. 483–95.

[4] conanexiles.gamepedia.com/Thrall

[5] conanexiles.gamepedia.com/Wheel_of_Pain

A nice but unfortunately very obscure example was the high quality but painfully unpopular MMO *Gods and Heroes: Rome Rising*.[6] One plausible analysis is that it was motivated by two conflicting goals: (1) to offer a culturally complex virtual world simulating late republican Rome as an amalgam of history and mythology and (2) selling exciting gameplay combat at a time when pure fantasy games were vastly more popular than historical simulations. An original version was developed by Perpetual Entertainment, which got as far as a closed beta test for the year beginning October 2007, then was shut down, and Perpetual went out of business. A *closed beta test* is an incomplete online version accessed by a small number of volunteer testers, who communicate with the developers about problems they encounter, and whose activity in the game can be observed by the designer as they develop a more final version for later commercial release. Seeing considerable potential in the game, a new company named Heatwave Interactive improved *Gods and Heroes* and launched a new closed beta test, which I joined as one of the volunteer testers on November 8, 2010.

The beta testing procedure was simply to play the game from level 1 to level 25, in my case over a period of nearly 6 weeks, and for my research rather than in my role as tester I took 2,222 screenshot pictures to record not only actions and environments, but also the quest-related messages that appeared on the screen, thus documenting the story in some detail. Often, at the end of a mission, a window with a brief questionnaire would appear on the screen, in one of two versions, allowing beta testers to communicate usefully to the game designers. One labeled "beta level feedback" would appear as soon as my avatar had achieved a new level of experience. It had a space where I could write a comment and three fixed choice questions I could answer by clicking one of five choices: (1) fun (from 1 = not fun to 5 = very fun), (2) difficulty (from 1 = very easy to 5 = very hard), and (3) length (from 1 = too short to 5 = too long). The other version came at the end of a specific quest, in the first case saying: "Congratulations! You have completed quest A Hero Rises: Call to Arms. To help us make the game better please provide feedback about this quest."

---

[6] godsandheroes.wikia.com/wiki/Main_Page

In addition to room for a comment and the three fixed-choice items just mentioned, these questionnaires included two items rating the particular quest: (4) reward (from 1 = valueless to 5 = very good) and (5) story (from 1 = farfetched to 5 = very good).

After improvements partly guided by the information and evaluations provided by the beta testers, *Gods and Heroes* launched commercially on June 21, 2011. I began multiple new avatars a few days later, intentionally on different servers, adding thousands of additional screenshots to my visual archive of the game. Of relevance here, a major construction component had been added, the family estate of the avatar that had been ruined in the recent warfare and needed to be rebuilt. The equivalent in the beta test version was simply a camp where the avatar could socialize with the avatar's minions. A key concept of *Gods and Heroes* was that the player's avatar is a Roman aristocrat who must assemble a team of NPCs who would perform various functions. Four of them could accompany the main avatar, serving as secondary avatars during combat, whereas the others would stay in camp. Most of the online communications about the game have vanished, but a forum at the MMORPG.com website survived, in which players discussed their hopes and experiences, over the complete history from April 2005 until July 2013. Simultaneously with the June 2011 launch, a thread of the forum discussed the estates, one of the players commenting:

> The estates were very recently added, at the start of beta we had camps instead, and a different back-story for them and your character, so info on them will be limited. They are still in transition, and not fully integrated with the rest of the game. The devs list a lot of things they will add to them after release, as to whether you will like them, depends on you, it's nice to have another part of the game to build on apart from your avatar, and minions, though I worry it will take away from having more useful social hubs, such as the capital.[7]

---

[7] forums.mmorpg.com/discussion/318652/anyone-here-can-explain-more-about-the-housing-estate-system-in-this-game

The estates were quite large, containing many buildings and a lake, framed by mountains. Minions who remained in the estate included a blacksmith who could make weapons and armor for the main and secondary combat avatars and a vendor who could buy loot from the main avatar and sell food and drink. The paper manual for *Gods and Heroes* explained further:

> Estates can be upgraded by performing quests given by the NPCs who live on your estate. A librarian, barracks commander, guard captain, house matron, and a Sacerdos will all be present on your estate and give you quests that can upgrade each of the buildings to which they are attached. The upgrade level of the buildings controls the rank of minions you are allowed to command. Higher level mystics will only work for you if your library is upgraded to a certain level. The same is true for skirmishers (Training Grounds), Defenders (Guard Tower), and Priests (Temple).

This is a very complex simulation of social construction of facilities. Very capable minions will work only for high-status aristocrats, and status can be gained by accomplishing goals desired by the workers associated with different buildings, each of which represents an institution of society. A player's video has survived on YouTube, describing the excitement that the estate could cause:

> I had just landed at my estate in Gods and Heroes and need to start building it up. I have quests to complete and as I do the buildings become rebuilt and new again. It really is massive, larger than Lord of the Rings Online's housing areas. I went over the hill and found MORE buildings. Every player has one, for free.[8]

The thralls in *Conan Exiles* and the minions in *Gods and Heroes* were somewhat limited in their apparent intelligence, so the best example to consider next is at the opposite end of the spectrum, NPCs that seemed to possess personalities.

---

[8] www.youtube.com/watch?v=CZuEBVKi7FI

Companions with Artificial Personalities

When *Star Wars: The Old Republic* launched in 2011, at any point in a high-level mission the user could select a secondary avatar based either on its skills and equipment or on its personality, which included the ethical system from which it would judge the behavior of the main avatar, becoming less helpful when it disapproved. Although not generally recognized as such, many of these options are forms of end user programming of AI assistants, which may be a standard feature of AI agents when they evolve into dynamic partners in a local community.

In the original virtual social structure, each SWTOR avatar would develop close relationships with five companions over the course of an extensive novel-like narrative, each having particular abilities and a distinctive personality. Each of the 2 factions had 4 separate avatar types, thus in total there were 8 narratives and 40 companions. A less significant avatar depicted as a droid (robot) served limited functions in the avatar's spaceship, one for each faction, thus bringing the total to 42. When a companion accompanied the main avatar on a mission, it would assist in moments of combat and follow the main avatar, thus exhibiting a low level of AI as it responded mechanically to events and avoided barriers while walking. On a far more sophisticated level, it exhibited simulated intelligence in development of its social relationship with the main avatar.

Often, at pauses in the action, a movie-like cutscene would appear on the computer screen, showing the main avatar and the companion in the presence of one or more NPCs involved in the mission, typically with a conversation between the main and an NPC. Often the player would have a choice to make, which could involve a life or death decision concerning the fate of another NPC. The companion would appear to listen to this discussion and form a judgment about the main avatar's decision, based on whether the companion personally likes or dislikes that kind of behavior. Over time, if the player makes decisions which the companion likes, the avatar will gain greater influence over the companion, who therefore will perform tasks more effectively. One of the SWTOR wikis explains the general features of this system:

> Companion characters will voice their perspectives from time to
> time, often giving information on current storylines and pointing

out locations to visit. They may also try to influence the player's decisions. Likewise, the player will influence each companion. The player's Influence on each companion is stored as a rank and the number of points accrued toward the next rank. More influence points are required to reach each successive rank. Each companion has likes and dislikes that apparently don't change throughout the game and the player's influence upon them will be increased by conversation choices and other choices that the companion either approves of or disapproves of while they are present. Giving appropriate gifts to the companion can also progress the companion toward the next influence rank.[9]

In many ways, the roles played by the companion changed over the years, as SWTOR was adjusted in an attempt to serve a wider audience. The original emphasis was on allowing the player to experience a complex, prescripted story, almost like being an actor in a new *Star Wars* movie. Each companion had a distinctive sidestory, some more complex than others, even involving missions for the avatar to complete. The variable measuring the companion's orientation toward the main avatar was called *affection*, and even defined by an SWTOR wiki in terms of human emotions, as "a scale that measures how the companion characters feel about the player."[10] The main stories would be completed at or slightly above level 50 of experience, and something like the original system still applies to avatars below that level.

In 2015, an expansion called Knights of the Fallen Empire added much higher level action, while removing the function of likes and dislikes after the original stories had been completed, and making many companions available to different classes of avatar.[11] Michael Branham's review of this expansion noted the redefinition of the companion–avatar relationship:

If you played SW:TOR before, you're used to thinking of companions and their Affection level. This Affection stat, affected

---

[9] swtor.wikia.com/wiki/Companion_Character

[10] swtor.wikia.com/wiki/Affection

[11] en.wikipedia.org/wiki/Star_Wars:_The_Old_Republic#Expansion_packs

by dialogue choices and gifts, gated companion story quests and romance options. Influence works similarly, but it ties into gameplay. For each rank of Influence you gain with a companion, you'll gain Presence (a stat which scales your companion's health/damage/healing) as well as time efficiency and critical rate for crew skill tasks. The crew skill portion is a nice bonus for crafting, but the Presence stat is the important part.[12]

A review by Leif Johnson noted that at lower levels the game became easier, and companions no longer served particular functions in combat:

Much of this ease springs from the changes to companions. KotFE's great shift is that they no longer have their own gear or specialized combat roles; instead, you can switch them between combat, healing, and damage dealing roles with a simple right click over their portrait. Playing as a Jedi Knight, that meant that all eight companions I met throughout the story focused on keeping me healed, which they did absurdly well.[13]

While occurring during combat, healing is effectively a specialized profession, comparable in some ways with resource gathering and manufacturing, and quite different in others. The obvious metaphor is the medical profession, and stitching up a wound while applying an antiseptic is a little like crafting. Depending upon the game, main avatars may be able to heal themselves by drinking a potion that had to have been bought or concocted earlier. Secondary avatars that can heal have limitations on how fast, continually, and effectively they can perform this function. In many cases, healer avatars either gain skills gradually as they do this job, over a period of weeks, or they can be trained through episodes with a trainer, or acquire equipment that increases their abilities. Training clearly employs

---

[12] Branham, M. November 3, 2015. "Knights of the Fallen Empire Review." *Ready:Set*. readyset.zam.com/article/36/knights-of-the-fallen-empire-review

[13] Johnson, L. December 10, 2015. "Star Wars: The Old Republic-Knights of the Fallen Empire Review." *IGN*. www.ign.com/articles/2015/12/11/star-wars-the-old-republic-knights-of-the-fallen-empire-review

at least the metaphor of AI, and skill improvement through experience does involve a simple form of machine learning, as the number in a particular memory register increases slightly whenever healing is performed.

Apparently, its designers changed SWTOR because they noticed that many players preferred unrestrained action, and personal relationships with the companion may have been unimportant for them. In addition, as was true in many MMOs of that period, the designers struggled to find ways to strengthen the economic returns. One consequence of this trend was a greater emphasis on buying influence over the companion by purchasing gifts from vendors, keeping in mind the companion's particular preferences. This could be classified as a shift from a psychoanalytic orientation to a behaviorist orientation, in the character of the simulated AI. Here we will emphasize the early days of SWTOR, given that the initial design was distinctive within the genre and yet well developed because it was an outgrowth of the simulation of moral decision making in the predecessor *Star Wars: Knights of the Old Republic*, a solo-player game dating from 2003.

To achieve a well-focused perspective on the rule-based AI of SWTOR's companions, Table 6.1 lists the seven Human companions that various kinds of avatar may have, within the Republic faction to which the Jedi knights belong. The classic *Star Wars* wiki, named Wookieepedia, called the Republic "a force of freedom and justice" and "a democratic union of sovereign star systems that governed the galaxy for a thousand years prior to the rise of the Galactic Empire."[14] The time frame referred to is the period before the original 1977 movie, but SWTOR imagines that thousands of years earlier the same two factions existed. Wookieepedia calls the Empire "an autocratic government" that imposed dictatorship "in order to preserve security and continued stability."[15] More simplistically, the Republic was nice and the Empire nasty or, in Jedi lingo, the Republic followed the Light Side of the Force, whereas the Empire followed the Dark Side. The information in Tables 6.1, 6.2, and 6.3 can be found inside SWTOR, but also in the online wikis.[16]

---

[14] starwars.wikia.com/wiki/Galactic_Republic

[15] starwars.wikia.com/wiki/Galactic_Empire

[16] swtor.wikia.com/wiki/Companion_Character;   swtor.gamepedia.com/Companion; starwars.wikia.com/wiki/Star_Wars:_The_Old_Republic

Table 6.1 Human companions of Republic avatars

Companion	Likes	Dislikes	Favorite Gift
Female			
Risha	Self-interest, profit, secrets, and new tech; romance	Unprofessional or emotional behavior, killing innocents, working with the stupid or uneducated	Luxury, underworld goods, cultural artifact
Kira Carsen	Confidence, bravery, kindness, morally correct actions; romance	Avoiding fights, weakness, disrespecting authority	Luxury, technology, underworld goods
Elara Dorne	Rules, propriety, selflessness; romance	Unnecessary violence, corruption	Luxury
Male			
Tharan Cedrax	Cleverness, logical thinking, aiding scientists, beautiful women, getting something for nothing	Mystical Jedi nonsense, force persuade, destroying science, heroism that involves danger	Luxury, technology
Felix Iresso	Republic military, leadership, danger for the greater good, honor and mercy; romance	Breaking the law, cruelty	Trophy, Republic memorabilia
Doc	Looking like a hero, romance and flirtation, helping those in need; romance	Looking bad, hurting the innocent, refusing to help	Luxury
Corso Riggs	Protecting the weak, being gentlemanly/ nice/polite toward women, punishing bad guys; romance	Hurting others for profit, hurting women (no matter what they have done), working with Sith, Imperials, or Separatists	Weapon, military gear

We can read a general Republic ethical culture into the likes and dislikes of these secondary avatars, notably a reluctance to harm innocent people, but we also see large differences among them that might be described as personality quirks. In terms of AI, the programming is preset, effectively as a large structure of if–then statements, and machine learning enters the picture only as the secondary avatar reacts to the key decisions by the primary avatar and the gifts received. Also, the personalities of the secondaries were selected by the SWTOR designers to interact in story-relevant ways with the nature of the primary avatar. The word *romance* was added to the list of likes when the companion was open to developing a romantic relationship with the main avatar.

For example, an SWTOR wiki reports:

> Risha is a companion of the Smuggler player character. She is also a potential love interest of the Smuggler. The player meets Risha when they acquire the space ship as part of the class quest. Risha will provide the player with more quests that are part of the smuggler class.[17]

The best-known smuggler in the *Star Wars* tradition was Han Solo, who possessed a good heart but was reckless, sarcastic, and somewhat cynical.[18] These characteristics represent one mode of adaptation to the fact that the Republic has failed to achieve its lofty expressed goals, marked by cases of government corruption and by a general disintegration of law and order. The things Risha likes, "self-interest, profit, secrets, and new tech," harmonize with this mode of adaptation and render her a logical "love interest of the Smuggler." Each of the eight SWTOR character classes has a potential love interest, among its five secondary avatars, Risha being the choice for male smugglers. If the player's smuggler avatar was female, then the potential lover was Corso Riggs, a man described by a different SWTOR wiki as "a cheerful, disarmingly optimistic mercenary soldier."[19] That wiki describes the nature of these computer-generated romances:

> Because all companion characters have personal speaking missions that appear after certain points in a character's story, there is sometimes the potential for some of them to become attracted to the character. If the player makes the decision to encourage those feelings, the companion will become a little more open to the player,

---

[17] swtor.gamepedia.com/Risha

[18] en.wikipedia.org/wiki/Han_Solo

[19] swtor.wikia.com/wiki/Corso_Riggs

and the potential for marriage becomes greater as the player levels up and gets closer to level 50. All classes have at least one male and one female companion that has the potential to become attracted to the player of the opposite sex. Some classes (such as the Smuggler and the Imperial Agent) have one or two other companions that could also have the same feelings, which leads to jealousy with some companions, and more exciting story lines.[20]

In *Star Worlds*, I compared the detailed life histories of Kira Carsen, a companion of Jedi knight characters, and Elara Dorne, a companion of a trooper character who shares the high values of a Jedi but lacks magical powers:

[Kira] had been taken from her parents at an early age because of her Force sensitivity and placed in a kind of child harem, where the emperor would possess her psychically from time to time, leaving her with memory gaps. After escaping while still quite young to Nar Shaddaa, the moon of Hutta dominated by criminal gangs, she lived by her wits and by building friendships with other refugees... Kira Carsen and... Elara Dorne, were similar in that both were decent, competent women who had begun life in the Empire but defected to the Republic. Elara Dorne had defected while an adult, so she had the British speech patterns possessed by all regular citizens of the Empire, an accent Kira had lost while a girl fugitive on Nar Shaddaa. Elara was exceedingly rule-oriented, so her defection was more rationalistic, even like a bipolar switch that had exactly two positions, Empire versus Republic, exactly following the rules of one or the other. She is not trusted in the Republic, despite her perfect service record.[21]

Table 6.2 lists the human companions of Empire avatars, beginning with Jaesa Willsaam, who has a different variant of faction ambivalence,

[20] swtor.wikia.com/wiki/Romance
[21] Bainbridge, W.S. 2016. *Star Worlds: Freedom Versus Control in Online Gameworlds*, 134. Ann Arbor, Michigan: University of Michigan Press.

acquiring a definite personality only within her story, seeking either honor on the Light Side of the Force or chaos on the Dark Side, which is also her only opportunity for romance.[22] Comparing Table 6.2 with Table 6.1, we see similarities and differences, rather than some simple distinction such as Republic = Good and Empire = Evil. These are individuals, and their diversity supports a complex narrative in which their life stories serve as chapters. Notably, not all of the companions capable of romance are listed, because some members of alien species are sufficiently humanoid to bond with people. For example, Ashara Zavros in the Empire is not listed in Table 6.2 because she belongs to the Togruta species.[23] It is worth noting that in 2015 it became possible for a main avatar to belong to the Togruta species as well, and the focus here on human companions merely keeps the analysis closer to the home planet where distributed manufacturing will be based.[24]

Many of the other secondary avatars belong to various intelligent alien species, but three are robots—or *droids* as *Star Wars* calls mobile intelligent machines—as well as one minor secondary droid avatar connected to the spaceship of each faction. *Droid* is a contraction of *android*, which the science fiction subculture used to describe *humanoid robots*. In Table 6.3, the T7-O1 astromech droid is most similar to R2-D2 in the movies, whereas the two starship droids are similar to C-3PO. Especially interesting is SCORPIO, a female robot—or at least a self-modifying robot who has taken feminine form the better to influence avatars—with a body both voluptuous and metallic.[25] The SWTOR interface describes her thus:

> Claims to have been designed for heuristic self-improvement by unknown parties. Current chassis is of recent design, suggesting multiple precursor bodies or independent database... SCORPIO places no inherent value on biological or cybernetic life and is

---

[22] swtor.wikia.com/wiki/Jaesa_Willsaam

[23] swtor.wikia.com/wiki/Togruta

[24] www.swtor.com/patchnotes/7222015/game-update-3.3-grand-togruta-celebration

[25] starwars.wikia.com/wiki/SCORPIO

Table 6.2 *Human companions of Empire avatars*

Companion	Likes	Dislikes	Favorite Gift
Female			
Jaesa Willsaam	Helping the weak, secrets of the Force, honor	Random cruelty, hurting innocents, rudeness	Republic memorabilia, cultural artifact, weapon, trophy, military gear
	Random cruelty, secrets of the Force, murder and chaos; romance	Honor, mercy, helping people	Weapon, luxury, military gear, trophy
Raina Temple	The Empire, the Sith, duty, honor; romance	Cruelty, casual violence, selfishness	Imperial memorabilia, military gear, Republic memorabilia, weapon
Male			
Andronikos Revel	Action, keeping promises, complications; romance	Authority, betrayal, backing down from a fight	Weapon, military gear, underworld goods
Talos Drellik	Artifacts, discovery, history, pro-Empire sentiment, clever word play	Cruelty, rudeness, secrets from allies	Cultural artifact, Imperial memorabilia, luxury, Republic memorabilia
Malavai Quinn	Patriotism to the Empire, rewarding hard work, honor; romance	Selfishness, betrayal, irrational behavior	Imperial memorabilia, military gear, weapon, technology, trophy
Pierce	Personal gain, hurting the Republic, danger and laughing at authority	Rules, kissing up, peace	Military gear, weapon
Vector Hyllus	Diplomacy, helping people, exploring alien cultures; romance	Greed, cruelty, prejudice, antialien sentiment	Cultural artifacts, Imperial memorabilia, luxury
Torian Cadera	Challenges, honor, Mandalorians, respect; romance	Selling out, cowardice	Trophy, military gear, weapon

Table 6.3 Droid (robot) companions of both factions

Companion	Likes	Dislikes	Favorite Gift
Republic			
T7-O1 astromech droid	Jedi, morally correct actions, defeating the Empire	Bullying, killing innocents, disrespecting authority	Republic memorabilia, cultural artifacts
M1-4X male war droid	Destroying the Republic's enemies, pro-Republic messages, courage	Anything against the Republic's goals	Republic memorabilia, technology
C2-N2 starship droid	None	None	Cultural artifacts, technology
Empire			
SCORPIO female war droid	Learning and gaining new tech, selfishness, killing threats	Self-sacrifice, duty, wastefulness	Technology, military gear, weapons
2V-R8 starship droid	None	None	Cultural artifacts, technology

interested primarily in self-iteration through rapid experience. If given appropriate challenges and upgrade opportunities, SCORPIO may prove cooperative for limited periods.

In the early history of SWTOR, it was possible and even necessary to obtain valuable weapons and armor for the companions as well as the main avatars. As companion–main relations simplified, that option was removed. In 2017, a player explained in a forum,

> Stats don't matter on any pieces of gear you give to a companion, including weapons. Some companion abilities require certain weapon types to be equipped in order to use the ability but the stats themselves on the weapons don't do anything, just like armor. Everything is cosmetic at this point (for companions).[26]

Given that SWTOR companions are technologically created entities, placing armor on one is an act of assembly, and creating the armor from raw materials is merely an earlier stage in a manufacturing process.

Personified Manufacturing Assistants

The role of artificially intelligent SWTOR companions in the manufacturing process increased over the years, even as their social role waned. Originally, a player could gather raw materials while exploring alien landscapes and battling monsters, then needed to go to a centralized facility where several specialized pieces of large machinery stood, such as a cybertech workstation shown visually in my earlier book, *Computer Simulations of Space Societies*. It shows a main avatar "making a synaptic awareness chip, from these raw materials: 4 units of fibermesh and 2 of bondite that he had obtained by scavenging, plus two bottles of brazing flux bought from a nearby vendor."[27] One of his companions would actually run the process, selected because it has high skills, but the main avatar must be present with the raw materials.

---

[26] www.swtor.com/community/showthread.php?t=910696
[27] Bainbridge, W.S. 2018. *Computer Simulations of Space Societies*, 214. Cham, Switzerland: Springer.

Years later, gathering raw materials from the environment could be done either by the main avatar or by companions, and the manufacturing would be done entirely by the companions without requiring the main avatar to be at any particular location, so long as the raw materials were in the avatar's bank vault or inventory. Most recently, economic tasks performed by companions included sending one away briefly to sell any junk in the avatar's inventory, and three main skill categories: mission, gathering, and crafting. For example, one of the mission categories is *investigation*, and one mission at level 7 of the 10 grades was Nonstandard Behavior Routines. Opening the crew skills interface and then the mission interface, I read: "On the planet Metellos, people are reporting their droids are wandering off for hours at a time—but always return, refusing to discuss their absence. Have your companion investigate." My companions were all at a high level 10 of influence, so which one I chose would not influence the outcome, but for narrative purposes M1-4X, the male war droid, seemed most appropriate. These companion missions all have financial costs, 2,075 credits in this case. It took M1-4X only 8 minutes and 4 seconds to complete the mission, but these investigations never tell the player what happened, other than success or failure. So, we did not learn why the droids were wandering off, nor did we see what M1-4X did on Metellos. In this case the mission was successful, returning one unit of transparisteel and slight improvement points to the status of the avatar.

Crafting activities involve companions but not the tiny stories of missions and virtual gathering. In *Computer Simulations of Space Societies* I explored how multiple avatars needed to cooperate in the manufacture of speeder bike vehicles of the appropriate style for each, so they could zoom in style across the surface of a distant planet:

> For example, the Vectron Speeder for an archaeologist would require an archaeologist to gather a certain number and type of artifact fragments and power crystals, and would appear to carry red, blue and green power crystals in the cargo space right behind the rider.[28]

---

[28] Bainbridge, W.S. 2018. *Computer Simulations of Space Societies*, 218. Cham, Switzerland: Springer.

All the stylish speeder bikes required 20 units each of farium metal and molytex compound, which could be obtained by the scavenging gathering skill. The bike for an archaeologist also required 10 midlithe gemstones, which could be obtained by the treasure hunting mission skill. In addition, manufacturing the bike required the cybertech manufacturing skill. However, no one avatar could possess four skills, so two or more would need to collaborate. High-level avatars can send multiple companions out on different gathering or mission activities simultaneously, at no reduction in cost but finishing a series of jobs more quickly. Thus, SWTOR encourages teamwork among simulated people as well as real ones.

The range of computational choices available to designers of simulated crafting social systems is well framed by comparing the series of developments in SWTOR with the rather unusual system in the original *Guild Wars*. Neither the main avatar nor a companion does the manufacturing work. Rather, an NPC at a fixed location produces the manufactured item, if given the necessary raw materials plus payment. For example, the first weapon maker the player is likely to encounter is named Arthur Ayala, who stands on the hill inside the city of Ascalon. He offers to make many different items, including an Ascalon longbow, which is more powerful than the bow that an archer is likely already to have. The labor will cost 100 gold coins, but also requires 5 wood planks from which the main part of the bow will be made.

The serious work involves obtaining the raw materials. Many MMOs allow avatars to chop down trees and saw boards from the logs, but peaceful gathering of wood planks was not possible in *Guild Wars*. The main avatar must obtain a salvage kit and use it to extract raw materials from items looted from dead enemies. Not far down the hill from Arthur Ayala stands an NPC merchant named Sanura, who sells a salvage kit for 40 gold coins. It may be used 10 times before it must be replaced. The most obvious way to obtain the wood planks is to salvage from old bows that are not needed, which can be collected by killing enemy archers.

That challenge reflects the fundamental fact that *Guild Wars* is a combat-oriented game based on teams usually having four members. Raw materials for crafting are not gathered peacefully from the natural environment, but taken from enemies. After the very first levels of experience, the enemies are far too dangerous for any one avatar to defeat. The example of a longbow connects to the class of avatar called a *ranger*, who not only is an archer but also can have an animal secondary avatar that can be ordered to attack an enemy, while the ranger shoots arrows at a distance. However, this pair of avatars is still rather feeble in combat, and counts as only one of the four in the standard quartet.

When playing with friends, or operating in an area where many other players are active, quartets of main avatars can form teams, plus whatever natural secondaries any of them may have. If a full team of main avatars is not available, the player may obtain the help of temporary secondary avatars called *henchmen*. In Ascalon, four of them are available, only three of which can be hired at a time, playing the four main combat roles of *Guild Wars* and appearing to have distinctive personalities, as suggested by their self-descriptions in the game:

Orion (male mage): "Maybe you've heard of me. I'm famous in these parts for my dazzling smile and my penchant for spectacular displays of fire magic. Women adore me. Other Elementalists want to be me. I'll tell you, it's tough sometimes being so well loved. Now, don't be shy. Just because I'm famous doesn't mean I'm not willing to help a fellow fortune seeker."

Reyna (female archer): "Most people call me 'Eagle Eye.' That's because I'm the best ranger this side of the Tarnished Coast. If you're looking for adventure, then you'll be needing someone to watch your back, someone who knows these lands like the back of her hand. My bow is at your service. Just say the word."

Alesia (female healer): "Call me Sister. All my friends do. I'm an adherent of the mystical arts and a follower of the mother goddess Dwayna. I'm skilled at healing magic and resurrecting those who fall during battle. As part of my training to become a high priestess in the church of Dwayna, the elders require that I offer my services to those who are in need."

Stefan (male fighter): "Are you here to just talk, or is there some real bravery in that gut of yours? My sword is sharp, my shield is strong, and I'm itching for a good fight. Are you going to stand there all day, or are we going to go find some trouble?"

It would be an exaggeration to say that these four henchmen actually have the personalities suggested by these prewritten texts, but they do harmonize with their functions in battle. If the player's main avatar is a ranger, then probably Reyna should not be one of the three selected secondary avatars, because she would duplicate the same role in the team's division of labor. As the main avatar walks across the war-torn lands, the team will follow, making their way around obstacles and standing near but not over each other. As they approach a team of NPC enemies, the player may begin the battle, for example, by shooting an arrow at the nearest of the foe. Or, the nearest enemy may detect the team's approach and spontaneously attack, other members of its team quickly following.

Stefan, the fighter, will rush forward and attack the enemy at close range. Orion will stand back and hurl fire. Alesia can also do some damage, but as soon as any member of the team is wounded, she will apply her healing powers. It is even possible that during a battle the main avatar will be temporarily killed, and she could revive him, with only a modest penalty to his strength. At times the team will be directly fighting more than one of the enemies, but often they will concentrate on the one the main avatar is aiming at. A constant worry is the safety of Alesia, because she cannot heal if she is dead, and some enemies are programmed to attack healers.

Once all local enemies have been killed, it is easy to loot whatever items may have dropped from them, which often includes coins, armor, weapons, and artifacts. For experienced avatars, more advanced salvage kits are available, and components used to upgrade existing armor or weapons may be found.[29] The *Guild Wars* wiki outlines this complexity:

> Certain items may have upgrade components attached that can be salvaged. These components can only be salvaged by using Expert, Superior, and Perfect Salvage Kits. When this is the case, a salvage component selection window appears, displaying all possible salvage components that can be salvaged from the item. The percentage chance of destroying the salvage item is shown for each

[29] wiki.guildwars.com/wiki/Upgrade_component

salvage component. Select the desired salvage component and confirm it (or cancel it to stop the salvage process). The salvage process always successfully produces the salvage component; only the salvaged item has a chance of being destroyed in the process. An item can be salvaged more than once if it still has salvageable components remaining and is not destroyed during salvaging. Salvaging for crafting materials always destroys the salvage item, as it translates to completely dismantling the item.[30]

A form of crafting rather like programming AI into a computer was central to the science fiction MMO *Tabula Rasa*. It was based on a set of intellectual concepts that made it very intriguing but also unpopular, and it lasted only from October 30, 2007, to February 28, 2009. Created by a team headed by Richard Garriott, son of an astronaut and the developer of the pioneer MMO *Ultima Online* that launched a decade earlier, who also produced *Shroud of the Avatar* a decade later, it promoted a spectrum of motives for development of real-world spaceflight.[31] The action takes place on two planets where refugees from Earth seek to build positive relationships with friendly aliens. Earlier publications have explored *Tabula Rasa* in some depth, and here we shall consider only one aspect: the tabula. In philosophy, psychology, and related fields, a variety of meanings have been attached to the concept of *tabula rasa* or *blank slate*. Any brief definition would be an oversimplification, but here the Wikipedia introduction is useful:

> Tabula rasa refers to the epistemological idea that individuals are born without built-in mental content and that therefore all knowledge comes from experience or perception. Proponents of tabula rasa generally disagree with the doctrine of innatism which holds that the mind is born already in possession of certain knowledge. Generally, proponents of the tabula rasa theory also favour the

---

[30] wiki.guildwars.com/wiki/Salvage
[31] Garriott, R., with David Fisher. 2017. *Explore/Create: My Life in Pursuit of New Frontiers, Hidden Worlds, and the Creative Spark*. New York, NY: William Morrow.

"nurture" side of the nature versus nurture debate when it comes to aspects of one's personality, social and emotional behaviour, knowledge and sapience.[32]

Each *Tabula Rasa* avatar has a tabula in its mind, which can be seen by the player as a window of the user interface, initially a grid of empty squares. As the avatar explores the two planets, a main goal is to find a series of *logos* shrines, where the avatar gains a new concept that is represented by an icon in a hieroglyphic language, that fills one of the cells in the tabula. The backstory explaining this within the mythos of the game is that a mysterious, advanced alien species called the Eloh has intentionally placed these shrines around the universe, so that diligent subsequent intelligent species could gradually gain their advanced culture. The name Eloh is quite meaningful. The Eloi in H.G. Wells' 1895 novel *The Time Machine* are the decadent elite descended from a scientifically advanced social class, but no longer have any understanding of the technology their ancestors created.[33] The Elohim in the Hebrew bible are gods, yet that is an ambiguous concept for monotheists, and it probably held different meanings at different times and places, and for different readers. Nearly a decade after the termination of *Tabula Rasa*, a specialized wiki still reports the fundamental assumptions:

> Thousands of years ago, an Ancient Species known as the Eloh, made a great discovery. They uncovered a key to a powerful science unifying all known theories of physics. With this key, they were able to unlock answers to the fundamental questions of the Universe that explain the nature of all matter and energy. This knowledge allowed them to develop Logos, a way to manipulate matter, energy, and force in unique and powerful ways. With the power of Logos at their disposal, they began exploring the universe. By folding space to quickly cross vast distances, they visited galaxies

---

[32] en.wikipedia.org/wiki/Tabula_rasa
[33] Wells, H.G. 1973. "The Time Machine." In *The Science Fiction Hall of Fame*, ed. B. Bova. 452–526. New York, NY: Avon.

of all sizes in a quest to meet other sentient life. The Eloh shared their knowledge with all whom could comprehend this powerful truth. But sharing such knowledge and giving other Logos-receptive beings the ability to manipulate matter, energy, and force would eventually trigger an intergalactic war between the Eloh and the Bane, resulting in the enslavement of many species and ensuring the Bane's place as our oppressors.[34]

Thus, the logos system can be used for good or evil, and the Eloh campaign to share their discoveries widely bears some similarity with this book's program to share insights that may facilitate the growth of local crafting. Certainly, the gradual diffusion after Hiroshima and Nagasaki of the secrets for making atom bombs endangered our planet, but it seems implausible that distributed manufacturing would have such dire consequences. Here, our focus is to understand the logos metaphor. Given that *Tabula Rasa* no longer exists, we must rely upon the printed instruction manuals, a few surviving online resources, and my own experience collecting all the logos available on the two planets.[35]

The logos shrines were not geographically random, but allowed an avatar who found all the shrines in a particular region to assemble them, plus earlier ones, into a functioning program that accomplished a specific goal. A pair of related examples involving battlefield creation of machinery is the turret and trap that can be made by an avatar of engineer class that has obtained the necessary logos plus ordinary raw materials. Here are the required logos hieroglyphs and descriptions from the manuals[36]:

---

[34] www.ign.com/wikis/tabula-rasa/Logos

[35] Bainbridge, W.S. 2011. "Science, Technology and Reality." In *The Matrix Online* and *Tabula Rasa*, 57–70.

Bainbridge, W.S., ed. 2010. *In Online Worlds*. Guildford, Surrey, England: Springer. 2011. The Virtual Future, 35–54. London: Springer.

[36] 2007. *Allied Free Sentients Field Manual*, 52. Pangyo, South Korea: NCSoft; Lummis, M. 2007. *Richard Garriot's Tabula Rasa*, 92–93. Indianapolis, Indiana: BradyGAMES/D.

Turret

Logos: Summon, Machine, Damage, Enemy

Description: "This ability is a major addition to an Engineer's lineup. You can deploy multiple turrets, each able to fire at enemies independently. Your enemies often spend time firing back at the turrets, which pulls some of the heat off your character. Aside from that benefit, the turrets deliver considerable damage to enemies in range."

Trap

Logos: Trap, Damage, Summon, Machine

Description: "Visually, this ability works the same way as Turret; your Engineer deploys a turret on the field that immediately starts to fire at enemies. However, the damage that Trap inflicts is very low. The purpose of this ability is to make enemies fire back at the false turret and destroy it. At that moment, the false turret discharges all of its energy into the aggressor, potentially killing the victim outright."

These two pieces of similar technology use only four logos each, three in common in the two sets. During action, the player does not need to state the logos in order, because once the full set of logos required for an ability have been collected, then the user interface contains an icon, here one for turret and another for trap, that may be placed in an action bar. Obtaining a logos at its shrine has a spiritual quality, expanding the mind and abilities of the avatar while filling in a cell in the tabula. Sending an avatar to a shrine can be an adventure in itself, but is functionally equivalent to a step in programming an AI. This action also requires geographic exploration, which deserves emphasis here because the following chapter is all about geography. An online *Tabula Rasa* wiki that still survives late in 2018 lists the locations of all the available logos, with their latitudes and longitudes, and information for each like that as follows[37]:

---

[37] tabularasa.wikia.com/wiki/Logos_list

Summon
Zone: Divide
Comment: "Inside cave at the top of the ruins. Requires: Friend (logos), Star (logos), Life (logos), Enlighten (logos), Here (logos)"

Machine
Zone: Pravus Research Facility (inside Wilderness)
Comment: "Just south of Southwest Fortification"

Damage
Zone: Wilderness
Comment: "In a cave in a cliff behind a group of Foreans"

Enemy
Zone: Wilderness
Comment: "Behind Imperial Valley"

Trap
Zone: Caves of Donn (inside Wilderness)
Comment: none

The Divide zone where the Summon logos could be gained is part of the Concordia continent of the planet Foreas, adjacent to the comparable Wilderness zone where Damage and Enemy can be found. Wilderness was the second zone visited by new avatars, ranging from levels 3 to 10 of experience on a system with a maximum of 50, while Divide was more difficult, ranging from levels 10 to 20. The class system in *Tabula Rasa* was structured as a tree diagram, branching at levels 5, 15, and 30, for example: recruit, soldier or specialist, sapper or biotechnician, demolitionist or engineer. Thus, a diligent explorer would have collected all five of these logos concepts before adopting the engineer specialty. Note that Summon requires already having collected five other logos concepts: Friend, Star, Life, Enlighten, and Here. The first four are also found in Divide and have no logos prerequisites, but the Here shrine was in Wilderness and required already possessing Mind and Power which also could be found in Wilderness. Of the five required for turret and trap, Damage was a prerequisite for entering the shrine where the War logos could be gained, and Enemy for the Victory shrine, both in Divide. Each logos was like a word that could be combined with others to form a functional sentence, and some sentences were required to obtain specific new words.

A Social System Integrating Human and Artificial Intelligences

The definition of AI blurs in online role-playing environments, because the user's own thought processes are deeply embedded in the system that processes information, but are not autonomous. Players act through avatars that impose constraints represented by the "skills" the avatar has acquired, and those skills are typically acquired in two ways: (1) by interacting with NPC trainers who are admittedly stupid but function as the interface to often complex parts of the programming and (2) through practice in which repeatedly crafting gradually increases a skill to the point where the player shifts to manufacture of a more advanced product to gain higher-level skill. In the socially very complex virtual world, *Elder Scrolls Online*, the social dimensions of simulated intelligence become obvious.

As Wikipedia notes, *Elder Scrolls Online* is a socially intensive extension of an exceedingly popular series of solo-player games:

> The series is known for its elaborate and richly detailed open worlds and its focus on free-form gameplay. *Morrowind, Oblivion* and *Skyrim* all won Game of the Year awards from multiple outlets. The series has sold more than 50 million copies worldwide.[38]

With respect to the online version, "In June 2017, it was announced that more than 10 million players had played the game since release, and that the game had around 2.5 million monthly active players."[39] Structurally somewhat comparable to *Dark Age of Camelot* on the large scale, each avatar in *Elder Scrolls Online* belongs to one of three competing factions with its own set of regions on a world called Tamriel, which at high levels

---

[38] en.wikipedia.org/wiki/The_Elder_Scrolls
[39] en.wikipedia.org/wiki/The_Elder_Scrolls_Online

of experience may battle each other in a central region that is contested among them. The multigame Elder Scrolls Wiki describes the geographic distribution of these complex alliances:

> The Aldmeri Dominion, situated in the provinces of the Summerset Isles, Valenwood, and Elsweyr.
>
> The Daggerfall Covenant, situated in the provinces of Hammerfell, High Rock, and Orsinium.
>
> The Ebonheart Pact, situated in the provinces of Skyrim, Morrowind, and Black Marsh.
>
> The province of Cyrodiil remains disputed, and is a constant battle-ground between the three alliances.[40]

Note that the names of some provinces duplicate the titles of earlier games in the series, reflecting the fact that all of them take place in the same imaginary world, but at different points in its long and rather medieval history. Whereas the three competing alliances separate the avatars and thus the player population into thirds, two kinds of guilds link across them: (1) factions of NPCs, each with a focus on a particular kind of action, some calling themselves "guilds," such as the Mages Guild and the Fighters Guild, and (2) the conventional guilds created by the players themselves. The latter kind of guild does function differently from, for example, in *World of Warcraft*. As in *A Tale in the Desert*, an avatar may belong to more than one, in this case with a limit of five. However, the memberships actually belong to the player, who may perhaps have three avatars, one in each faction, that wind up belonging to the same five guilds. In such a case, the player may have chosen one combat guild with alliance to each of the Aldmeri, Daggerfall, Ebonheart Pact factions, plus two peaceful guilds that are oriented to economic production and commerce.

The Mages Guild and the Fighters Guild are not really at war with each other, but represent distinct cultures and areas of technology. I had studied *Elder Scrolls Online* twice before, most recently in 2014, and I

---

[40] elderscrolls.wikia.com/wiki/Alliances

returned in 2018 to study the complex crafting and commerce system, using a high-level Ebonheart character who happened to have saved a good deal of virtual currency to invest, and was situated at Davon's Watch, in the region of Stonefalls, Morrowind, a large city with headquarters for both the Mages and the Fighters. Each of these guilds manages training in three crafting professions that harmonize with its culture. A message obtained from an equipment crafting writs bulletin board said: "Interested parties should seek Millenith at the Fighters Guild for Blacksmith, Clothier, and Woodworker certification. Speak with Danel Tellano at the Mages Guild for Provisioner, Enchanter, and Alchemist certification." Here are simplified statements of what each of these six professions produces:

Blacksmithing: weapons and armor using metals
Clothing: armor from animal materials and plants
Woodworking: bows, staves, and shields
Provisioning: food and drinks
Enchanting: glyphs to enchant other items
Alchemy: potions and poisons

The two guild headquarters were a short distance apart, with the six facilities for doing the crafting and places to buy and sell situated between them and to the south, all inside the city walls. Ingredients needed for the novice training missions could be gathered just outside the walls. Millenith and Danel Tellano each offered training in the three crafts related to their guild, and the player could select one, or, as I did, perform all six. Each is in a series of steps, as the specialized wiki page explains:

Talk to Millenith.
Acquire Iron Ore.
Search for Iron Ore.
Talk to Millenith.
Search Rocky Areas for Ore if you run out.
Acquire Iron Ingots.
Talk to Millenith.
Craft Iron Dagger.

Deconstruct a Blacksmithing Item.
Talk to Millenith.[41]

The first meeting with Millenith is at the Fighters Guild headquarters, but the later encounters in that sequence are at the crafting station for blacksmiths. In the first meeting with her, the player selects choices in a text-based conversation, in which her words are also spoken aloud by a voice actress, that begins:

Millenith: "You here for crafting certification? Don't worry, there's no cost involved—your alliance covers all my fees. Once you're certified, they'll let you fulfill the crafting writ. Everyone wins!"
Avatar: "Yes, I saw the notice. How do the crafting writs work?"
Millenith: "They're daily requests for crafted goods, but they're only available to certified crafters. If you can show me you know your craft, I'll get you certified."
Avatar: "All right. Tell me how this works."
Millenith: "I can train and certify blacksmiths, clothiers, and wood-workers. If that sounds like something you'd want, we can get started."

Thus an avatar can earn wealth and experience doing daily crafting of specified items at the direction of the automatic system operating the crafting writ bulletin board, but it is also possible to sell miscellaneous crafted items to NPC merchants, or to other players. The next step in the conversation is for the player to decide if Millenith should describe each of her three professions, send the avatar over to her friendly competitor Danel Tellano at the Mages Guild to discuss in the same way the three other professions, or start training such as in blacksmithing.

Millenith: "Prove your way around a forge and I'll certify you. But you have to commit. I can only train one discipline at a time."
Avatar: "I want to be certified as a blacksmith."

---

[41] elderscrolls.wikia.com/wiki/Blacksmith_Certification

Millenith: "I want you to craft a simple iron dagger. First you'll mine some iron ore, then refine the ore into iron ingots. You'll use those ingots to make the dagger."

Avatar: "You'll certify me if I make an iron dagger?"

(after producing ingots at a forge):

Millenith: "Go to the blacksmithing station and craft an iron dagger. Nothing fancy—you shouldn't need more than two iron ingots. Oh, and you'll need a style material. You can purchase them from any blacksmith, or scavenge them yourself, if you're thrifty."

(after producing the dagger):

Millenith: "Next is deconstruction. You learn a lot when you break something into parts, even more so when it's someone else's work. Go deconstruct your dagger—or anything else, really. As long as you do it at a blacksmithing station."

Avatar: "How is deconstruction helpful to me?"

Millenith: "You'll regain some components, of course—but the real trick is to deconstruct another crafter's work. You can learn far more by disassembling someone else's material than your own."

The *style material* referred to is a necessary ingredient that can take different forms, each of which gives the product a different visual appearance but the same function. The avatar starts out able to make products in the right style for personal use but can learn other styles by obtaining and reading the appropriate *motif* book. During ordinary adventuring and combat, avatars loot weapons and armor from NPC enemies, which they can deconstruct, often thereby learning how to make products of the same kind. Crafting and deconstruction earn experience for the avatar, and completing quests can earn general skill points which can be invested in crafting abilities or in other strengths.

In five of these crafts, alchemy being the exception, it is easy to invest skill points to obtain a *hireling* who will automatically obtain a small supply of raw materials each night, and is represented as a specific person, but only through the equivalent of e-mail messages rather like the chronological opposite of the crewmember missions in SWTOR, telling the end of a little story rather than the beginning.

Another form of hireling is a *guild trader*, an NPC who stands in the vicinity of crafting stations and can effectively be rented by a guild to sell products produced by its members. In any bank, a member of a guild can access a private market where members of a guild sell valuables to each other, indeed checking what is for sale from each of the avatar's possibly five guilds. But the only way to buy from a guild to which one does not belong is through a guild trader.

On the Massively Overpowered blogsite, Eliot Lefebvre asked, "What MMO has frustrated you the most with trading restrictions?"[42] Several players quickly criticized *Elder Scrolls Online* for lacking a centralized auction house, not perhaps noting how the social structure was programmed to emphasize cooperation within and across guilds. Like Millenith and other interactive NPCs, the words of virtual merchants can be heard as well as read, and a wiki that lists 197 of them standing at many locations observes:

> All guild traders in base game zones, as well as Hew's Bane and the Gold Coast, use shared sets of six dialogue lines based on their race. Interestingly, only seven races are used for these cases (leaving out the human races other than Redguard) and each race has only one gender. This is perhaps to reduce the amount of voice acting required.[43]

Conclusion

To be sure, we cannot predict what aspects of local manufacture will employ new forms of AI or the extent to which simulated intelligence will feature in the human–machine interface. Conceivably, designers of distributed manufacturing technologies will study AI's manifestations in MMOs to gain ideas and inspirations for developing the future interfaces and may even program their own simulations as part of the design development and testing. In any case, the NPCs in MMOs are important parts

---

[42] massivelyop.com/2018/10/28/the-daily-grind-what-mmo-has-frustrated-you-the-most-with-trading-restrictions/

[43] en.uesp.net/wiki/Online:Guild_Traders

of the social simulations, often performing specialized roles that players were unprepared to take, such as boring jobs selling materials or managing a bank. Indeed, in the cases of both the original *Guild Wars* and *Star Trek Online*, companions often function as substitutes for human team members, when friends are not available to accompany the player on a mission. An unanswerable question relevant throughout this analysis is where on the amateur–professional dimension most forms of local production will be. If AI and related information technologies reduce the significance of human expertise, then it is possible that even complex forms of manufacture will be accomplished by semiprofessionals operating machines possessing a degree of intelligence and communicating with their operators by means of a human-friendly interface.

CHAPTER 7

Large-Scale Technical and Cultural Variation

With the earlier chapters as background, the concluding chapter will consider the large-scale structure of virtual worlds, which typically exists on several levels. Most of these worlds consist of multiple regions, each of which may support a local community of nonplayer characters (NPCs) to which, in some cases, people may also belong. Connected sets of regions may function as nations or factions. For example, in *World of Warcraft*, the main Human city is Stormwind, on a temperate seacoast, whereas the Dwarves concentrate in a city named Ironforge in a less hospitable region to the north. But both belong to the Alliance faction, in competition with the Horde, and Stormwind is connected to Ironforge by an underground railway. Two classic examples dating from 2001, *Anarchy Online* and *Dark Age of Camelot*, divide their worlds into multiple regions organized in three competing factions, rather than just two. All popular MMOs exist in multiple forms, supported on separate Internet servers, differing by time zone, by language, and in the specific rules governing human interaction, notably more or less violent. The MMOs differ greatly in how their internal economic systems connect to the economy of the wider world, notably in the extent to which users pay only a standard subscription fee or buy advantages inside the MMO using money from outside.

Thus the virtual local communities are both separate from but also within a much wider and complex virtual civilization, as the local communities of our own real world will be in the coming years. Commercially successful MMOs tend to add territory over the years of their profitability, chiefly to keep veteran players active, by providing additional interesting activities and environments, thereby motivating them to pay subscriptions or continue to buy virtual goods. A game that stops growing fades from public awareness, both because the gamer news sites feature it less often and because players do not encourage friends to join them in new group missions. Regions of a gameworld primarily differ in how experienced and thus both skilled and well-provisioned an avatar must be, which seems unlikely to model the meaning of geography in our real world. However, spatial variation is often used as a metaphor for social, cultural, and economic variations, such as the "fields of science," "sectors of the economy," and "social distance." Most MMOs depict conflict between ethnic or political coalitions, each having some home territory, which could represent the areas served by competing Internet providers as well as it does nation states. Typically, each virtual faction has a distinctive culture, whether framed in terms of race, religion, or revolutionary ideology. We might prefer the local manufacturing of the future to be independent of any of these traditional human conflicts, but to some degree they may be unavoidable.

The Structure of Open Virtual Geographies

A good example to begin with is a virtual world that is about to go out of existence, erasing all its geography from human experience, with limited exceptions like this description that had been copied into a wiki that may survive for a while:

> Nexus itself is wild and unsettled, with an endless variety of dangerous frontiers just waiting to be explored. Crumbling Eldan ruins lie hidden within majestic forests, towering mountains, and murky swamps, containing arcane magic and ancient technology of unimaginable power. The rusting wrecks of giant robots lie half-buried in shifting desert sands, and strange and deadly alien creatures prowl in the shadows of extraordinary monolithic machines. And hidden among all of these wonders are the dark secrets of the Eldan themselves, and the answers to why they disappeared from planet Nexus so long ago.[1]

---

[1] wildstar.gamepedia.com/Nexus

This was the nexus for complex interactions between human beings, in the MMO *WildStar*, and connected a score of rather large regions, with gateways between adjacent regions and air-taxi services. Like *World of Warcraft* and many other MMOs, avatars were divided into two factions, the Dominion and the Exiles, each of which controls some of the regions designed for avatars at low experience levels. In an earlier book chapter devoted entirely to *WildStar*, I explained the structure and function of the early-level geography:

New players begin in a tutorial set in outer space, on an *arkship*, then select one of two starter regions in which to enter Nexus. The initial choices for the Dominion are Crimson Isle and Levian Bay, while for the Exiles they are Northern Wilds and Everstar Grove. These are very earthlike but somewhat wild lands that serve as advanced tutorials. There are 50 levels of general experience advancement in *WildStar*, the first 3 levels being earned easily on the arkship, and levels 4 through 6 gained through very active missions in a Nexus starter zone, that would be challenging for anyone who is not an experienced MMO player, but are not especially difficult for veteran players. Each of the four starter regions leads to a second separate region: Crimson Isle to Deradune, Levian Bay to Ellevar, Northern Wilds to Algoroc, and Everstar Grove to Celestion. These four routes take avatars to experience level 15, and their geographic diversity supports different story-based quest arcs, motivating players to create multiple characters, thus paying subscription fees longer, or buying more virtual goods for real money.[2]

At this point in their process, avatars gain easy access to their faction's huge capital city, Illium in the case of the Dominion and Thayd in the case of the Exiles. These are centers of commerce and industry, and many players do their virtual manufacturing at extensive sets of simulated machinery, near NPC vendors, including a pair representing the

[2] Bainbridge, W.S. 2017. *Dynamic Secularization: Information Technology and the Tension between Religion and Science*, 185. Cham, Switzerland: Springer.

two parallel player markets, one primarily for raw materials and the other for products. The next full region dominated by the Dominion is Auroria, and the Exiles hold Galeras, both of which are good for farming and gathering raw materials. Higher level regions are contested between the two factions, which the *WildStar* wiki describes thus:

> The Dominion is a powerful interstellar empire that rules the galaxy, using military strength, religious fervor, and advanced weaponry and technology. Established by the Eldan more than a thousand years ago, the Dominion has now claimed Nexus as its own—and will stop at nothing to ensure that the fabled planet is completely under their control. Having recently arrived in force, the Dominion is prepared to crush the ragtag alliance of the Exiles, unleashing the full power of their formidable military against those who would dare trespass upon the sacred ground of planet Nexus![3]
>
> The Exiles are a gutsy group of mercenaries, refugees and exiles that have forged an unlikely alliance upon the planet Nexus. Scattered beyond the edge of known space by the violent expansion of their sworn enemy, the Dominion, the races of the Exiles have now banded together to explore the wonders and face the dangers of Nexus, hoping to make a new life among the planet's mysterious ruins and unexplored frontiers. United by a burning hatred of the Dominion, the Aurin, the Granok, the Mordesh, and the Humans of the Exile Fleet are prepared to make a final stand against the invading empire that has claimed the planet. The Exiles consider Nexus their last hope, and they are willing to die for it.[4]

Note that these two paragraphs not only explain the contest between the two factions, but also express the meaning of the geography to them, "sacred ground" or "last hope." Manufacturing in *WildStar* was exceedingly complex and included a selection of six tradeskills, five of which

---

[3] wildstar.gamepedia.com/Dominion
[4] wildstar.gamepedia.com/Exile

produced products to help avatars during their adventures: armorer (heavy, metal armor), outfitter (medium, leather armor), tailor (light, cloth armor), technologist (medical supplies), and weaponsmith (weapons).[5] The sixth production tradeskill was architect, who crafted a wide variety of objects that can be added to a player's home, which was located in the faction's capital city, was unusually important in this particular MMO, and was capable of extensive customization, as the housing article in the wiki explains: "You start off with simple designs and can build them up into more desirable designs with different features, the inner outer, walls, roofs, doors, windows, wallpapers and furniture can all be changed or added onto your home."[6] Table 7.1 documents the series of 21 special architecture quests completed by one of my Dominion avatars, on the way to total mastery of this profession. Each quest was obtained from a work order board in a particular region, but usually the manufacture was done in Illium, then the product was delivered back to an NPC at the same location where the quest was obtained.

The first example, producing five metal platforms, can explain the general process. The mission to make these products was obtained in one of the early Dominion regions, either Deradune or Elevar, that are designed for avatars of experience level 6 to 14. Each tradeskill began by giving the avatar a small number of simple schematics, conceptualized as the computer program used by the production equipment to manufacture a particular product. Schematics to make the items in Table 7.1 could be gained by manufacturing earlier items in a very complex network of 128 schematics, while also increasing the avatar's general skill in a 6-rank system: novice, apprentice, journeyman, artisan, expert, and master. The required raw materials, 25 iron chunks in this case, could be obtained by a gathering tradeskill like mining in the same region where the quest was obtained or purchased from other players through the marketplace in the capital city.

As the wiki explains, "The schematic for Metal Platform is a variant of the Metal Plank schematic."[7] This means that making a platform

---

[5] wildstar.gamepedia.com/Tradeskill

[6] wildstar.gamepedia.com/Housing

[7] wildstar.gamepedia.com/Metal_Platform

Table 7.1 A series of region-specific architect quests to manufacture home products

Region	Product	Schematic	Raw materials	Rank	XPS	Vouchers
Deradune or Ellevar 6–14	5 metal platforms	Metal plank	25 iron chunks	Novice	10	211
	5 bramble bushes (small)	Bramble bush (small)	10 knotted heartwood, 15 bladeleaf	Novice	16	316
	3 long fences (Granok)	Short fence (Granok)	25 iron chunks	Novice	27	474
Auroria 14–22	5 Galeras walls	Crude fence	15 knotted heartwood, 10 iron chunks	Novice	40	342
	5 single metal crates	Airtight container	20 titanium chunks, 5 ironbark wood	Apprentice	66	513
	5 wicked fire totems	Moodie totem	25 ironbark wood	Apprentice	110	770
Whitevale 22–28	5 medical cots (hovering)	Medical cot (hovering)	25 titanium chunks, 5 zyphyrite crystals	Apprentice	40	342
	5 snapping traps	Snapping trap	25 platinum chunks, 5 hydrogem crystals	Journeyman	66	513
	5 marauder lamp post	Bronze lamp post	20 platinum chunks, 5 hydrogem crystals	Journeyman	110	770
Farside 28–34	3 purple star pillow piles	Comfortable pillows	15 whimfibers, 6 reinforced leather	Journeyman	80	556
	3 wall-mounted generators	Holovision set	6 platinum chunks, 6 hydrogen crystals	Journeyman	132	834
	2 fuel pumps	Easycrank panel	4 platinum chunks, 2 diamonds	Journeyman	220	1,251

Wilderrun 35–40	3 shiphand lockers	Burnished treasure chest	9 augmented hardwood, 9 xenocite chunks	Artisan	80	556
	3 fancy dressers (Dominion)	Dresser (ornate)	15 augmented hardwood, 3 xenocite chunks	Artisan	132	834
	2 triple wall dividers (honey)	Wall dividers (honey)	6 xenocite chunks, 6 augmented hardwood	Artisan	220	1,251
Malgrave 40–44	3 chests (gold)	Skinny-waisted barrel	12 augmented hardwood, 6 xenocite chunks	Artisan	160	903
	3 peeping eye security cameras	Chua spotlight	12 xenocite chunks, 6 shadeslate crystals	Artisan	265	1,355
	2 coffee tables (heart-collection)	Heart-collection side table	6 primal hardwood, 4 denimite, 3 galactium chunks	Expert	440	2,033
Grimvault 45–50	3 Tiki torches	Tiki torch	12 primal hardwood, 6 augmented leather	Expert	0	1,467
	3 nautical wheels	Nautical chair	9 primal hardwood, 6 augmented leather, 3 galactium chunks	Expert	0	2,201
	3 Freebot surge protectors	Dreg wind-well	9 galactium chunks, 9 primar hardwood, 3 starshards	Expert	0	3,303

required special action while using the plank schematic in a manufacturing device. The user interface displayed a circular design space, defined by two orthogonal dimensions, aesthetic versus function and organic versus synthetic. A small circular area somewhere in this space was marked for each variant of the main schematic, and the user must purchase and apply as many as three additives, as explained by this text in the interface: "Use additives to move your target into the green zones to uncover recipe variants!" The player needs to experiment, as well as analyze, to figure out which sequence of additives will give the greatest probability of success. Delivering the required product back to the region where the quest was obtained would give two rewards, an increase in architect experience (XPS) and crafting vouchers, which the wiki explains: "A crafting voucher is a form of currency obtained from work order quests. These vouchers are used to purchase tradeskill schematics, crafting materials and tradeskill talent respecs."[8]

If *WildStar* simulates a future economy, *A Tale in the Desert* simulates an ancient one, but in a way that suggests how distributed manufacturing may indeed require differentiation of social organizations across territory. There are, of course, many reasons why production of the same goods at different locations might be organized differently, including (1) natural differences in available raw materials, (2) issues of transportation over long distances, (3) regional social and political conditions, and (4) explicit territorial separation such as represented by independent nations. *A Tale in the Desert* incorporates all of these factors.

As Chapter 3 explained, *Tale* is unusual in that it cycles through a repeated simulation of building ancient Egypt called a *telling*, each taking about 2 years. Egypt is divided into many regions, but the main geographic variable is latitude, the distance north or south roughly along the river Nile. In the eighth telling a new feature was introduced, three ethnic factions, the Meshwesh in northern Egypt, the Hyksos in central Egypt, and the Kush in southern Egypt.[9] Upon entry, players must select membership in one of these three, and most will seek to gain prestige within it, although there is an option to change factions later on. Very early in each

---

[8] wildstar.gamepedia.com/Crafting_voucher
[9] atitd.wiki/tale8/Factions

telling, players set up guilds, and each player may belong to several. To set up one of these groups, avatars must build a guild hall at a geographic location of their choice, with the implication that it will belong to the faction that dominates that area. Players do not fight each other, but compete peacefully, claiming additional territory for their faction.

To offer a clear picture of this system, on June 2, 2018, I visited the guild halls of all the large guilds I could locate, obtaining a list of members from the hall's information interface, while simultaneously accessing the avatar search system within the general interface. I found 17 guilds with at least 35 members each, for a total of 511 avatars, in most cases representing one player each given that *Tale* does not have classes and every avatar can experience all dimensions of Egyptian life. Of these 511, 119 belonged to Meshwesh, 246 to Hyksos, and 146 to Kush. Table 7.2 arranges the guilds by latitude from north to south, using *Tale's* mapping system that employs *coords*, each of which represents a subjective meter or two. So, the simulated Egypt is much smaller than the original, but still large, perhaps 20 kilometers north to south.[10]

Many of the guilds are revivals of ones from previous tellings, which explains why two are much larger than the others, zFree and KaPoW. The wiki page for zFree says:

> Our guild is most importantly a social hub for members. zFree aims to provide the facilities that enable us all to achieve our individual and collective goals, including regional research. We are a large guild, so it is important that we all follow some Common Guidelines.[11]

A wiki page lists zFree's guidelines concerning proper behavior, ending: "If in doubt, please ask a guild elder. In-game you can see a list of elders by typing in '/info zFree' in the chat area, then clicking on the Members tab."[12] KaPoW's wiki pages stress the practical means for making products, such as the locations of mines and natural resources and

---

[10] atitd.wiki/tale8/Maps
[11] atitd.wiki/tale8/ZFree
[12] atitd.wiki/tale8/ZFree/Common_guidelines

Table 7.2 *Major guilds in a simulated Egypt*

Guild name	Latitude of hall	Member avatars	Interlocks		Faction membership		
			KaPoW	zFree	Kush	Hyksos	Meshwesh
DIMWITS	7234	41	0	2	0	1	40
Ritual Tattoo Guild	7036	40	2	7	2	11	27
Meshwesh Research Initiative	7036	40	0	1	0	0	40
PKURFL4X	4817	40	0	1	1	0	39
Alpha	2355	39	1	7	1	37	1
zFree	2287	147	12	147	13	131	3
Safari Club	2080	87	14	45	16	63	8
Shroomers of the Darkest Night	2080	68	10	32	12	48	8
Acro Maniacs	2080	36	5	16	6	30	0
Our Land!	2020	52	0	28	0	52	0
Vigils	1490	52	1	25	2	47	3
Amigos	-974	79	1	27	4	72	3
Les diamants du Nil	-980	45	0	11	1	38	6
Wretched Hive of Scum and Villainy	-1799	35	22	13	22	12	1
The BFG (Big Friendly Guild)	-3738	50	22	14	23	15	12
Garden of Eden	-6000	51	36	15	42	6	3
KaPoW	-7111	133	133	12	132	1	0

of the guild's storage and manufacturing facilities: "You can always help by donating: Wood, Clay, Charcoal, Jugs, Papyrus seeds, Linen, Canvas, Rope, Metals, Ores, gems, Insects, Salt, Acid, Coconuts, Sulphurous Water."[13]

The second and third columns of data in Table 7.2 show how many avatars belong to zFree and KaPoW, as well as to the guild represented by the row in the table. Just 12 avatars belong to both of the two largest guilds, and the largest numbers of interlocks for both tend to be at roughly the same latitude as the big guild. The three columns of data at the right show that the members of guilds do tend to belong to the same faction that dominates their third of Egypt. However, membership in two of the guilds is really not local, but they do communicate information that has geographic character. Safari Club operates a text chat where members can tell each other where specific animals can be hunted at the moment, and Shroomers of the Darkest Night does the same for collectable mushrooms.

The Structure of Closed Virtual Geographies

In contrast to the open-world structure of *A Tale in the Desert*, some MMOs consist of a very large number of separate environments, some of which exist simultaneously in multiple versions and thus are correctly called *instances*, but others of which merely serve specific functions without doing so in multiple forms. The classic example is the original *Guild Wars*.[14] As Wikipedia explains:

> The Guild Wars universe consists of persistent staging zones known as towns and outposts. These areas normally contain non-player characters that provide services such as merchandising or storage. Other NPCs provide quests and present rewards to adventurers. These areas are also used when forming groups of people to go out into the world and play cooperatively. Players that venture out from the staging area and into an explorable area

---

[13] atitd.wiki/tale8/KaPoW/projects
[14] en.wikipedia.org/wiki/Guild_Wars

are then able to use their weapons and skills to defeat monsters and interact with other objects in the game. As players progress through the game, they gain access to additional staging zones. Players can then transport their characters instantly from one staging area to another using a process commonly referred to as "map traveling."[15]

An extreme recent example is *Shroud of the Avatar*, as it was explored in 2018. At that point in its history, one rather large continent was open, plus islands of various sizes. It is quite common for virtual worlds to add new territory, in expansions that also add story-based quests and experience levels, but *Shroud* is an extreme case because it was open to some players very early in its development, because its funding largely came from contributors to a Kickstarter campaign launched in 2013 by Portalarium, the development company, and from early purchases by players.[16] The largest island, named Hidden Vale, was the first area available, during pre-alpha testing, December 12, 2013, through May 25, 2014.[17] The starter area when I began in July 7, 2018, was a place called Solace Bridge Outskirts, in Perennial Coast on the southeast corner of the main continent, Novia.

There were three locations along the border of Solace Bridge Outskirts where one could leave that area, jumping to the *world map*, which was represented symbolically as a miniature territory across which the avatar could walk, with tiny trees, towns, and adventuring areas of various difficulty levels.[18] To enter a town or adventuring area required clicking on a small sign in the air representing its entrance. Each adventuring area was identified as belonging to a difficulty *tier*, from 1 to 5, and survival required advancing one's avatar high up the experience ladder before entering a tier 4 or 5 area. While walking along a road in the world map, one would occasionally see an enemy or animal, and coming close would hurl one into an *encounter*, the equivalent of a mobile adventuring

---

[15] en.wikipedia.org/wiki/Guild_Wars

[16] en.wikipedia.org/wiki/Shroud_of_the_Avatar:_Forsaken_Virtues

[17] sotawiki.net/sota/Hidden_Vale

[18] sotawiki.net/sota/Novia_regions; www.shroudoftheavatar.com/map

area. Mountains ringed the Perennial Coast on the north and west, and there were only two obvious paths through them, Brightbone Pass and Eastridge Gap, but both were lethal tier 5, and two hidden routes I also discovered were equally dangerous.

There was a safe way out of the Perennial Coast, however, a *lunar rift* that was inside Solace Bridge, a tier 1 adventuring area very near Solace Bridge Outskirts. These lunar rifts are clearly an adaptation of the *moongates* in *Ultima Online*, the predecessor of *Shroud of the Avatar*. There were eight of these across the regions of the world, and the one in Hidden Vale was located in a city named Owl's Head.[19] Each lunar rift was a small version of Stonehenge, with a glowing ball of light at the center, and a bolt of lightning firing toward one of eight standing stones, each representing one of the possible destinations. The lightning slowly moved from one stone to another, taking fully 70 minutes to complete a circuit. Jumping into the ball of light would teleport the avatar to the corresponding destination, so often one was forced to wait a long time if a particular location were the goal. When the lighting focused on the stone representing one's current location, the teleport would still work, but the destination was random. Thus, it was difficult, but not impossible, to explore all of the continent before reaching a very high level of experience.

Some story-based quests required travel, and also one could gain 100 coins of the game's currency the first time one visited any town. A dynamic online map offered information about all the instanced locations, so efficient exploration required walking one's avatar everywhere, while also checking information in the map's database and a list of towns in a wiki.[20] A sense of the range of destinations available is conveyed by Table 7.3, which lists the major categories of fixed locations in the Perennial Coast. NPC towns offered many services, and both kinds had lots where players could place houses of various styles and sizes.

Given that Shroud was constantly under development, the actual list of towns was constantly changing, so Table 7.3 counts only those I could actually find on August 25, 2018. Some player-operated towns had either

---

[19] sotawiki.net/sota/Lunar_Rift

[20] www.shroudoftheavatar.com/map/; sotawiki.net/sota/Perennial_Coast

Table 7.3 *Locations confirmed by exploring the Perennial Coast*

Type of instance	Number	Names
Tier 0 Adventuring	1	Solace Bridge Outskirts (starting location)
Tier 1 Adventuring	1	Solace Bridge (contains lunar rift)
Tier 2 Adventuring	5	East Perennial Trail, South Celestial Wetlands, West Perennial Trail, West Veiled Swamp, Whiteguard Foothills
Tier 3 Adventuring	5	Desolate Hills, North Celestial Wetlands, Solace Forest, South Brightbone Woods, Spectral Mountains
Tier 4 Adventuring	4	Approach to the Shuttered Eye, North Brightbone Woods, Restless Woods, Spectral Foothills
Tier 5 Adventuring	5	Brightbone Pass, East Veiled Swamp, Eastridge Gap, Necropolis Barrens, Spectral Mines
NPC Town	11	Aldhaven, Aldwater, Ardoris, Celestis, Grayacre, Highiron, Lochfield, Redmill, Shadowmist, Solania, Soltown
Player Town	15	Artemis Outland, Enclave, Glenraas, Hameln, Hometown, Knight's Bastion, Mithril Underdarc, Niven-shire, Oceania, Outlander Welcome Center, Refugees Haven, Seers Sanctuary, Sidus Clarum, Tahr Al'ard, Wolves Den

been removed or renamed. According to a wiki page, there were two kinds of towns operated by players:

> Player run towns are the locations in the game that are controlled by Portalarium but populated, nearly exclusively, by the Avatars. There are usually not going to be quests and there will not be Gathering nodes or Monsters in these towns, unless they are under siege. Players can freely, and safely, live in these towns as long as they can pay their rent. Player owned towns are the locations in the game that were paid for by a player and added to the game by Portalarium. The player that purchased the town controls who has access to lots. At any time the town owner, or town stewards, can kick players from their lots.[21]

The user interfaces of most well-developed gameworlds include maps of the territories, often becoming visible step-by-step as the player explores, or readily available from the beginning. Physical books of maps, comparable to atlases, were published in connection with the launch of MMOs that publishers expected would be very popular, such as *Star Wars the Old Republic Explorer's Guide*. Explicitly referring to itself as an atlas, it begins:

> It's light years from Alderaan to Voss. If you get stuck on Tatooine, you'll end up a shriveled husk amid the desert sands if you don't know where you're going. Every *Star Wars: The Old Republic* player needs an atlas; one that displays every zone on every planet is essential for novice and expert alike. After a brief rundown on all the game's classes, the atlas is organized in alphabetical order by planet. Within each map chapter, you will find four main map types: world, enemy, zone, and interior maps.[22]

---

[21] sotawiki.net/sota/Community:Towns

[22] Searle, M. 2011. *Star Wars the Old Republic Explorer's Guide*, 3. Roseville, California: Prima Games.

Enemy maps mark areas where specific groups of enemies concentrate, whereas zones are large outdoor areas defined by a cluster of quests as well as by geographic features. Interior maps outline indoor instances. Each planet is an instance, comparable to a different Internet server, even offering players a list of avatars belonging to the same faction currently active on that world. But planets in space-oriented science fiction MMOs are not the largest possible geographic units. *Star Wars: The Old Republic* simulates only one galaxy, but it is divided into five regions: Coreward Worlds, Seat of the Empire, Hutt Space, Distant Outer Rim, and Unknown Regions.[23]

Transformed Real-World Geographies

Many solo-player computer games are set in real-world locations, such as Washington DC for *Fallout 3* and Boston for *Fallout 4*, which are role-playing games, or the *Total War* series that are strategy games recreating specific historical battles, in which the player operates an entire army rather than just a single avatar, on a simulation of the original battlefield. *Defiance*, an MMO set in the San Francisco area, has multiple connections to the real world but is set at a time in the near future when civilization has collapsed, which is also the premise of the *Fallout* games. The violent transformation of our real world as it became virtual in an MMO can be seen as an extreme metaphor for the fact that information technology is changing the meaning of geography, if not exactly as Peter Goldmark, quoted in Chapter 1, hoped it would. *Defiance* was connected to the 38-episode television series of the same name, set under the same social conditions but taking place in the ruins of St. Louis. Many games have been based on television programs, notably the *Star Trek* series, but *Defiance* was unusual in that the game launched simultaneously with the TV program, and for a time there were joint promotional activities.

According to the backstory, a colonization fleet of spaceships arrived at Earth in 2013, under the mistaken belief that our planet was uninhabited, and their multispecies passengers called Votans could make it their

---

[23] swtor.wikia.com/wiki/Galaxy_Map

new home. Attempts to broker peace failed, and the Votan technology intended to adjust Earth to resemble one of their home planets went wild:

> While the Votans had intended to use their terraforming technology in a carefully planned manner, the Arkfall haphazardly unleashed chaotic and radical changes to the biosphere and even the geology of Earth, making the planet dangerous to both humans and the aliens. The earth was scorched, chasms opened in the ground, new mountain ranges were raised, and the surface of the planet was covered with dust and debris.[24]

The consequence for San Francisco was equivalent to a rise in the sea level, with many local disruptions of roads and other structures, even as some fragile landmarks such as the Golden Gate Bridge survived. Notably, Silicon Valley has become an island, completely separated from the mainland. The game contains a convenient map system; another map with many of the locations marked exists online (but dated from the game's launch and lacking Silicon Valley), and both can easily be compared with real-world maps.[25] The player enters *Defiance* in an area slightly northwest of Mount Tam (Tamalpais), and the main area east and south contains regions named Madera, Marin, and Sausalito, Madera in this case not being the city of that name that is far inland, but taking its name from the nearby town of Corte Madera. Much of a player's early work consists of doing story-based missions across these four regions while increasing skills, armor, and weaponry. Then it becomes possible to cross southward into the heart of San Francisco, which like Silicon Valley is now an island.

Early levels of experience involve a rich story having connections to the television series which include the occasional appearance of NPCs representing its main characters, Joshua Nolan and his adopted alien daughter, Irisa Nyira. But after the beginning, the nature of the action shifts primarily to randomly occurring *arkfalls*. As a wiki devoted to both the game and the TV program explains, a vast ring of shattered spaceships

---

[24] en.wikipedia.org/wiki/Defiance_(TV_series)

[25] www.ign.com/maps/defiance/world

now circles the Earth, called the Ark Belt, so chaotic that debris is constantly falling to Earth:

> Common arkfalls are intermittent meteorite showers caused by falling debris from the Ark Belt. This includes everything from cargo pods to entirely intact sections of an Ark. These arkfalls can bring precious resources, alien technology, and sometimes nasty forms of life to the planet's surface.[26]

In the game, arkfalls almost always deliver nasty aliens, some of them intelligent warriors, but also many monsters. Main goals of the game are to kill these enemies and loot their corpses of valuable resources.

The arkfalls occur essentially at random and are immediately marked on the in-game map, so players rush to the location and instantly collaborate with each other, without the need of any prior social organization. The company that developed *Defiance*, Trion Worlds, had included a similar feature in its earlier and more conventional MMO, *Rift*. Note that this special feature gives *Defiance* and *Rift* very dynamic geographies, with the consequence that social organization is also dynamic. One implication is that much local manufacture in future years will also be dynamic, frequently changing the nature of the products and the social organizations producing them, supported by agile communication technologies. An early online review raised an issue very relevant for the theme of this book:

> My biggest complaint about Defiance is the fact that there is no crafting system. I know, I know; I can hear you say "not every MMO has to have crafting." Well, you sir are wrong. A semi post-apocalyptic world certainly warrants the need for crafting and trading, especially when there is rampant talk about crystals that are necessary for power and plants that have special chemicals in them. If Defiance had some form of crafting, it would give the game the needed variation in gameplay that it currently lacks.

---

[26] defiance.wikia.com/wiki/Arkfall

Actually, *Defiance* does have crafting, just of a very different kind from that found in more conventional games that have less emphasis on very rapid action. Resources gathered at an arkfall can be sold and often salvaged, which means taking them apart to obtain components. A portion of the "EGO" interface specifically serves the salvage function, as this in-game message explains: "This EGO extension allows for the modifying of weapons and for the salvaging of old components. The salvage matrix can be used to upgrade items, breakdown items, attach mods, and remove mods." At random I just now selected one of many looted weapons that happened to be in my avatar's inventory, an assault carbine. Right clicking allows me to see that I could earn 250 coins by breaking it down to resources. I could also attach a mod, remove or retrieve one, and for 1,000 coins I could even add a mod slot. The inventory also contained a large number of looted mods, including a good collection of different scopes that could give guns greater accuracy. Placing a scope on a gun is a legitimate form of crafting, albeit a simple action. A page of the IGN game-oriented website offered an initial overview of the four kinds of mods that could be added to weapons. "Stock Modifications usually affect stability," and IGN listed 12 examples. "Barrel Modifications usually affect accuracy" (21 examples). "Magazine Modifications usually affect reloading or ammo capacity" (20 examples). "Sight Modifications usually affect accuracy and will replace your zoom with a scoped zoom (similar to a Sniper Scope)," with 15 examples, many of which were in my inventory.[27]

The insights relevant for real-world distributed manufacturing should be obvious: Even though our main focus should be on complex systems for producing diverse products, very significant portions of the future economy may be much more specialized. Under conditions in which the surrounding socioeconomic environment is changing rapidly, simple production systems may be more adaptive than complex ones.

Another real-location game, Xsyon, deserves close study, for being a rather pure *sandbox*, lacking many prescribed quests or other story aspects, yet offering a rich world where residents may create their own

---

[27] www.ign.com/wikis/defiance/Modifications

homes and fortresses. The location is Lake Tahoe at the California–Nevada border, similar in geography to the real place, but lacking ruins of today's settlements and containing two small but prominent islands. There are two Xsyon servers, one named War for player-versus-player combat and one named Peace where cooperation is favored. Wikipedia explains the main principles of this virtual geography:

> The edge of the playable world is surrounded by a toxic green mist, which will kill players which venture too far into it, and causes animals to mutate. The zones have varying Danger Levels depending on the types and amounts of hostile creatures in the zone. The Danger level generally increases as you move away from the center of the map toward the mist. Players claim protected areas of land by forming a tribe and placing a totem.[28]

In my earlier book, *Virtual Sociocultural Convergence*, I offered a cultural analysis:

> We can reasonably speculate that *Xsyon* is intended to be pronounced *Zion*, which is the name of the last redoubt of human civilization in the *Matrix* movies, in addition to having many traditional religious and utopian connotations. The *Xsyon* wiki describes the situation in five words: "Modern technology has consumed itself."[29] The avatars prowl the resultant rubbish heaps, while feeling some affinity to the Native American cultures that had preceded industrialism. Yet the gameplay requires the user to gather material resources, create tools, produce more and more products necessary for life, and gain technical skills. Thus, *Xsyon* is the rebirth of technological civilization, potentially recapitulating William F. Ogburn's theory of technological determinism. In so doing, it places in the foreground of the experience a set of activities that a very large fraction of more popular MMOs place in the

---

[28] en.wikipedia.org/wiki/Xsyon

[29] www.xsyon.com/wiki/index.php/Category:Xsyon_History, accessed May 17, 2014.

background. Thus it is an excellent virtual world in which to learn about resource gathering and crafting.[30]

Technological determinism is the widely influential theory that the main driver of history is technological invention. In 1776, Adam Smith argued that investment in technological innovation would reduce the amount of human labor required to produce goods.[31] In 1813, Robert Owen analyzed the impact of the industrial revolution, arguing that it required new perspectives to guide the creation of better forms of society.[32] In 1857, Herbert Spencer asserted that technological development followed laws similar to those governing biological evolution.[33]

In his 1922 book, *Social Change*, William F. Ogburn modeled history as a sequence of four constantly repeated steps: (1) invention, (2) accumulation of inventions that could be combined to make new inventions, (3) diffusion of inventions both geographically and from one area of human endeavor to another, and (4) adjustment which often involved *cultural lag* as the institutions of society took time to adapt to the changed technological circumstances.[34]

Of course, there are alternate theoretical perspectives. Beginning in 1776, the same year as Smith, Edward Gibbon published the massive *History of the Decline and Fall of the Roman Empire* that argued societies could overextend themselves, seeking to achieve more than they practically could, in the Roman case producing centuries of glory followed by a thousand-year Dark Age.[35] Gibbon's erudite rival of the 20th century, Arnold Toynbee, published a dozen books arguing that the fate of

---

[30] Bainbridge, W.S. 2016. *Virtual Sociocultural Convergence*, 29–30. London: Springer.

[31] Smith, A. 1812. *An Inquiry into the Nature and Causes of the Wealth of Nations*, 133. London.

[32] Owen, A. 1813. *A New View of Society*. London: Cadell, and Davies.

[33] Spencer, H. 1857. "Progress: Its Law and Causes." *The Westminster Review* 67, pp. 445–85.

[34] Ogburn, W.F. 1922. *Social Change with Respect to Culture and Original Nature*. New York, NY: Huebsch.

[35] Gibbon, E. 1880. *History of the Decline and Fall of the Roman Empire*. New York, NY: Hurst and Company.

any society was largely determined by how well its elite responded to challenges, with collapse being the likely but not inevitable long-term outcome.[36] Over these years, many serious authors have contemplated the possibility that our own civilization was fated to fall, including Oswald Spengler, Pitirim Sorokin, James Burnham, and Patrick Buchanan.[37] Our third example of a postapocalyptic virtual world, *Fallen Earth*, has this rather sophisticated backstory:

> The *Fallen Earth* story begins in the 21st Century, when the first in a series of natural disasters hits the United States. As Americans struggle to recover, an investment tycoon named Brenhauer buys a controlling stake in a mega-corporation named GlobalTech. By 2051, he moves his headquarters to the Grand Canyon Province, where GlobalTech eventually creates a self-sufficient economic and military mini-state. Meanwhile, in India and Pakistan, the Shiva virus, named for the dance-like convulsions that it caused in its victims, appears among the human populace. As the infection starts to spread, countries accuse each other of engineering the virus. Political paranoia turns to open aggression and nuclear conflict. The nuclear conflict combined with the virus devastates the planet. Less than one percent of Earth's population survived the Fall, and the Hoover Dam Garrison and Grand Canyon Province are the only known outposts of human civilization. Outside the protective confines of the Hoover Dam Garrison, the player encounters ruins of the old world, genetically altered creatures, strange technology, and six warring factions. Some factions seek to rebuild the old world, others wish to build a new one in their own image, and some simply desire chaos and anarchy.[38]

---

[36] Toynbee, A. 1947–1957. *A Study of History*. New York, NY: Oxford University Press.

[37] Spengler, O. 1926–1928. *The Decline of the West*. New York, NY: A. A. Knopf; Sorokin, P.A. 1937–1941. *Social and Cultural Dynamics*. New York, NY: American Book Company; Burnham, J. 1964. *Suicide of the West*. New York, NY: John Day; Buchanan, P.J. 2002. *The Death of the West*. New York, NY: St. Martin's Press.

[38] en.wikipedia.org/wiki/Fallen_Earth

For earlier projects I ran one avatar throughout *Fallen Earth* to explore the entire territory and all kinds of action, then added two others specifically named for two of the main theorists of civilization collapse, Oswald Spengler who was a violent avatar and Pitirim Sorokin who was dedicated to peaceful advancement through technology.[39] Originally, the six warring factions were organized in a complex circle, each having one mortal enemy at the opposite side of the circle, two less intense hostilities with the two factions on either side of the main enemy, and two potentially friendly factions nearby on the circle. Later during the years when I periodically returned to *Fallen Earth*, the system was simplified to just three pairs of mortal enemies, without alliances between factions:

> Children of the Apocalypse (Anarchy, Chaos): The CHOTA work to destroy the remains of the old world to create a new world where all men are free.
> At war with:
> Enforcers (Order): The Enforcers labor tirelessly to restore law and societal standards in a world where chaos and death reign.
> Lightbearers (Spirituality, Society): The Lightbearers are mystics, healers, and warriors, united on a quest for harmony and peace.
> At war with:
> Travelers (Profit, Self): The Travelers do what it takes to get the most benefit with the lowest cost, even if that means breaking a kneecap or two.
> Vistas (Balance, Nature): The Vistas work to create a harmonious existence between humankind and nature.
> At war with:
> Techs (Technology, Science): Only by restoring the scientific accomplishments of the old world can the new world be saved.

The terms in parentheses are taken from various wiki pages, and the descriptive sentences are taken from within the user interface.[40] Geographically, this world is divided into a series of ever more difficult

---

[39] Bainbridge, B.S. 2016. *Virtual Sociocultural Convergence*, 211–35. London: Springer.
[40] fallenearth.wikia.com/wiki/Factions

sectors, which map onto the territory in Arizona near the Grand Canyon. Sector 1, named Plateau, is right beside the Grand Canyon and lacks forts belonging to the warring factions, presumably to give new players time to adjust before making serious decisions about faction affiliation. Embry Crossroads is the largest town and may represent Prescott, Arizona, because it is surrounded by many crashed aircraft, and Prescott is the home of Embry-Riddle Aeronautical University.

Each of the high-level sectors has a town for each of the six factions, offering allied avatars a few quests and facilities for crafting and economic exchange, and guarded by NPCs who will kill any enemy avatar who approaches. There is also a barter town, which in the second sector is named New Flagstaff after the city of Flagstaff that is northeast of Prescott. The *Fallen Earth* wiki says: "There are currently 4 sectors, with 4 additional pseudo-sectors, one of them being PvP-only."[41] The four regular sectors have separate bases for the six factions, while the pseudosectors have more distinctive sociogeographic structures:

Sectors:
Plateau—levels 1 to 15
Northfields—levels 16 to 30
Kaibab Forest—levels 31 to 46
Alpha County—levels 50 to 55
Pseudosectors:
The District (Territory Control)—PvP "sector"
Deadfall—levels 45 to 50
Terminal Woods—levels 45 to 50
Epsilon Zone (The Outpost)—levels 50 to 55

Note that a player who merely seeks to ascend to the experience level cap of 55 would naturally go through the first three regular sectors, then climb five levels in either Deadfall or Terminal Woods, before returning to finish in Alpha county. Kaibab is a real forest in Arizona, and Deadfall is described as a county of Kaibab, containing a town that seems to have

---

[41] fallenearth.wikia.com/wiki/Category:Sectors

taken its name from the Los Alamos laboratory in New Mexico that played such a key role in development of the atomic bomb:

> The capital city of Los Alamos offers access to Sector, Barter, VIP and Utility vaults; as well as a myriad of crafting material vendors, craft trainers and skill vendors. However, some skill books are notably absent, such as Group Tactics, Social and lower level First Aid. All towns in this sector are faction neutral with the exception of Tabara which will be hostile to players that do not have sufficient Shiva's Favored faction.[42]

Shiva's Favored is a seventh ideological faction, with which an avatar can develop a positive relationship. They are mutant humans who cannot survive without chemicals that would be toxic to ordinary humans, so they intentionally seek to pollute the environment. They are at war with another faction that calls itself Shiva's Blessed, and both take their name from the Shiva virus that was so significant for the fall of civilization, and itself was named for Shiva, the destroyer god in Hinduism.

A sense of more local geography can be gained by considering where an avatar needs to go in and around New Flagstaff to accomplish various kinds of manufacturing. Several blocks of ruined buildings surround a park that contains a LifeNet pod used for fast teleport travel, outside which are standing two NPCs, Edward Gadbaw the stable manager and Chase Ricketts the garage manager, who can take care of any horse or vehicle the player does not plan to use for a while. On one side are bank vaults, a mailbox, and NPC Rodney Hassle who is the local auctioneer. Players buy and sell not only products they have made, or raw materials they harvested, but also a very large number of books that an avatar needs to read (consume) in order to gain specific skills and other abilities. NPC merchants specializing in 4 of the 11 tradeskills are standing at a gazebo nearby: Chelsey Camps (geology), Tori Tryon (medicine), Ines Bigby (mutagenics), and Kylan Heidelbrecht (nature). Trainers for their tradeskills are only a couple of blocks away in the

---

[42] fallenearth.wikia.com/wiki/Category:Deadfall

ruined city. An Armorcraft workshop is at the southwest edge of the park. Across the street outside the west corner of the park stands the weaponry workshop, where Karter Jennett sells books that teach how to make swords, knives, axes, hammers, and other tools. A merchant named Yugene Quinn sells some of the raw materials for making these products, although they can also be harvested from the environment or obtained from other players. One of the simplest tools, a utility knife, requires just four pieces of scrap iron, whereas a pitchfork requires seven pieces of scrap iron plus five pieces of salvaged wood. Down the street to the northwest can be found a lab for the science tradeskill, a ballistics workshop, and a cooking facility.

Outside the east corner of the square stands Donny McNabb, the construction trainer and a construction foreman who explains what this tradeskill is all about. Here is the conversation this NPC had with my avatar named Sorokin, in which Sorokin's words were fixed choices selected to move the conversation along:

> Foreman: Hey! Careful, Sorokin, this is a construction area. Or will soon be. We've been working on methods to do more than just restore old buildings and live in them, and you can be part of the effort if you like.
>
> Sorokin: Sure, how's this work?
>
> Foreman: Well, you get some instruction manuals and tools from my friend here to get the basics. Before you move up to anything fancy though, you'll want to start small with stuff like campsites.
>
> Sorokin: Tell me how camps work.
>
> Foreman: Camps are very simple. You have to make construction materials out of the junk you'll be scavenging in your travels and use them to put together tents and basic fortifications. Honestly, if you've ever built an ATV or put together a gun, the principle is the same: get parts, refine them, then put them together to get the end product. You following so far?
>
> Sorokin: Cool. What kinds of camps can I build?
>
> Foreman: We've got the tools and the knowledge to help you put together simple camps with fires and tents and such, but we've also

gotten with the Bankers, the Riders, and all those whacky warring factions to come up with some fancy stuff...

Sorokin bought from Donny McNabb a Camps 1 instruction book for 10 coins and a construction kit for 50. A construction workshop stood very near the park, but he could also build components anywhere, the workshops merely speeding up the process. For example, a wooden support could be made anywhere at a rate of 1 per 15 minutes, whereas the time in a workshop was only 11 minutes and 15 seconds. There was in fact no equipment in the workshop, and Sorokin did not need to do anything with his hands, so except for the delay this construction procedure was entirely implicit. At first, he had the skill only to make wooden supports, but at skill level 15 he could also make cotton canvas, and then as he progressed "bundles" for four of the low-level structures: campfire at skill 30, pup tent at 45, and both firing range and training dummy at level 60. Here are the materials required:

Wooden support: five scrap wood, one weak adhesive
Cotton canvas: six ragged cottons
Campfire bundle: eight scrap woods, seven scrap coals, three ragged cottons
Pup tent bundle: six wooden supports, two cotton canvases, two scrap fasteners
Firing range bundle: six wooden supports, four cotton canvases, two scrap papers, two scrap fasteners
Training dummy bundle: six wooden supports, four cotton canvases, four frayed cottons, one scrap fastener

There are several different sets of construction products, including four levels of camps, each requiring the avatar to acquire and use a tradeskill manual. The introduction in the *Fallen Earth* wiki explains:

Construction allows players to construct "Campsites" and their components. Campsites are one-shot items that occupy an area and give various buffs to nearby friendly players. Campsites last for 3 hours in general, and buffs gained from them increase in efficiency as time is spent in the area... Harvesters and Farms are used for producing materials.

Another one of my avatars had constructed a farm that produced the raw materials for cooking.[43] Here are the applications of the four camp bundles, quoted from the in-game interface:

Campfire bundle: This camp creates a warm fire which boosts your stamina regeneration.

Pup tent bundle: This camp creates a simple tent that makes you rested, increasing health regeneration for 1 hour, and the bonus improves depending how long you remain at the camp.

Firing range bundle: Remaining at the camp grants you a bonus to firearm skills for 1 hour.

Training dummy bundle: Remaining at the camp grants you a bonus to Melee, Dodge, and Melee Defense for 1 hour.

One avatar may activate only one bundle at a time, for example, starting a campfire. Note the range of metaphors associated with buffs in general: clothing, jewelry, potions, magical spells, and here location near a constructed camp. As an avatar advances in general experience, it gains points that can be invested in the "stats," such as dexterity and will power, that set limits to the avatar's abilities. Whereas perception is of some value for the tradeskills, the most important stat is intelligence.

Sociocultural Geography in the Original *EverQuest*

One of the earliest gameworlds, dating from 1999, *EverQuest* has one of the most finely differentiated systems of classes and number of races, plus an exceedingly rich polytheistic mythology, practically defining the fantasy genre. It also provided a conceptual map of the finely differentiated social system. In its heyday, a sufficient number of avatars were constantly being created, by old and new players alike, that it made sense

---

[43] fallenearth.wikia.com/wiki/Category:Construction

for them to originate at different locations in the virtual geography. In the earlier years, and even today at lower levels of avatar experience, the races and thus cities were categorized in terms of three alignments: good, neutral, and evil. For example, the natural home for Dark Elves was Neriac, an underground city considered by players to be the "evil capital" of Norrath.[44]

In ancient days on our real Earth, polytheism offered a prescientific conceptual scheme for categorizing primarily three classes of things. First, each deity may personify a particular phenomenon of *nature*, as Poseidon and Neptune signify the waters of the sea and Gaia represents land or the earth. Second, some deities represent aspects of human *psychology*, as Ares and Mars symbolize the aggression of war and Loki (or Loge) is unreliability or even deceit. Third, a deity may be a tribal totem, as Jehovah began his existence as the god of the ancient Hebrews, thus geographically located. All three dimensions were incorporated in the *EverQuest* mythos, in a way that allows us to analyze how they fitted together.

Online social media offer a great variety of means by which to conduct quantitative social science comparable to censuses and questionnaire surveys, and a good source for *EverQuest* data is the online guide ZAM, also known as Allakhazam's Magical Realm.[45] When players registered at ZAM, data could be ported over from *EverQuest* itself about the Internet server, race, class, experience level, and deity of their avatars. In October and November 2017, I downloaded data about all 33,833 avatars for which all these variables were recorded. The method was somewhat laborious and very careful, working with a search page of the Allakhazam website.[46] One could, for example, search for all the Half-Elf Druid avatars who worshiped the rain deity Karana, and the displayed results would be a list of avatars giving all the variables except deity on a row of text.

In order to explore how geography correlates with culture, a reasonable way to summarize the research results is to consider the three factions of deities separately: Good, Neutral, and Evil. These terms have somewhat unconventional meaning, because avatars in all three factions

---

[44] everquest.wikia.com/wiki/Neriak

[45] en.wikipedia.org/wiki/Allakhazam

[46] everquest.allakhazam.com/db/charsearch.html

regularly violate norms against killing and stealing, slaughtering vast numbers of NPCs including animals and innocent citizens of communities the player's avatar does not happen to be friendly with. Unlike more recent virtual worlds, like *EverQuest II*, the original *EverQuest* does not offer the player precise information about the avatar's reputation with the large number of local factions encountered, only giving vague text like "Scowls at you ready to attack!" versus "Regards you as an ally." But the reputation ranges are the same for all three player factions, thus giving Good and Evil avatars equal numbers of mortal enemies and friends. The chief differences I observed are two: (1) The Evil starting area and home cities are dark, gloomy, and populated by horrors, whereas the Good ones are bright and pretty. (2) The philosophical concepts associated with the deities are different, with Neutral being rather more sophisticated than either Good or Evil.

Table 7.4 lists the 5 Good deities, reporting their 13,837 adherents, who are 40.9 percent of the total. Most popular is the Goddess of Nature, or Mother of All, named Tunare. More than half of her 9,046 adherents are Wood Elves, and the other races with more than 10 percent are High Elves and Half Elves. Both High Elves and Wood Elves naturally belong to the Good faction, but the four other races listed in Table 7.4 are by nature Neutral: Half Elf, Human, Froglok who are humanoid amphibians, and the unusually intelligent humanoids who call themselves Erudites. In general, members of the Neutral races have the option of becoming Good or Evil, depending upon the major choices they take.

Among Tunare's adherents, almost exactly half are either druids or clerics, two of the priestly classes. Another large fraction, rangers, are a hybrid class especially oriented toward Tunare, described as "warriors attuned to the ways of nature, able to call upon the power of the wild to aid them in their fights."[47] The other deity-class connections are similarly meaningful. Quellious is a pacifist child goddess, and thus it superficially makes sense that a majority of her followers are monks. Yet this class is somewhat violent, using martial arts techniques and thus representing the popular-culture stereotype of Asian kung fu experts who remain calm

---

[47] www.everquest.com/classes

Table 7.4 The Good deities of EverQuest

Deity	Title	Adherents	Main races	Main classes
Tunare	The Mother of All	9,046	55.3% Wood Elf 26.6% High Elf 12.3% Half Elf	36.8% druid 29.3% ranger 14.6% cleric
Mithaniel Marr	The Truthbringer	2,042	43.8% Human 24.6% Froglok 12.9% Half Elf 10.6% High Elf	44.7% paladin 12.1% cleric
Quellious	The Tranquil	1,574	59.7% Human 32.1% Erudite	58.8% monk
Erollisi Marr	The Queen of Love	712	38.9% Human 29.1% High Elf 22.1% Half Elf	23.9% paladin 20.6% enchanter 16.2% bard 11.5% cleric 10.4% magician
Rodcet Nife	The Prime Healer	463	73.9% Human 20.3% Half Elf	37.4% paladin 36.5% cleric

while in combat.[48] The fact that the god Rodcet Nife is called The Prime Healer obviously draws clerics to him, given that their primary social function is healing wounded teammates. Paladins are a hybrid class, who wear heavy armor and directly battle foes, yet they alternate with healing their teammates when that function is needed.

The 10,486 adherents of 7 Neutral deities, listed in Table 7.5, are 31.0 percent of the total 33,833 avatars. I like to think that Karana and The Tribunal represent the ambivalent nature of reality, Karana being the forces of nature that simultaneously create and destroy and The Tribunal being the judicial processes of humanity that carefully weigh evidence pro and con. In the *EverQuest* theology, both Dwarves and Gnomes were created by the Neutral deity Brell Serilis. Dwarves belong to the Good faction but are drawn to their god because of their cultural tradition of mining beneath the ground, and he is The Duke of Below, sanctifying the caverns and tunnels beneath the surface of the Earth. Like the Gnomes, the Drakkin are Neutral, related to Humans but having a touch of dragon blood. The Dark Elves belong to the Evil faction, which means they can easily ally themselves with a Neutral god, but not a Good one. It is possible to obtain a magical scroll to change an avatar's race or deity.[49] Of the 3,246 Dark Elves in the dataset, just 17 converted to the worship of a Good god, compared with 249 who had gone Neutral without the need for such a scroll.

Note that four of these deities seem to symbolize the traditional four elements: Brell Serilis (earth), Karana (air), Solusek Ro (fire), and Prexus (water). Karana is not the water god, merely because his title mentions rain, because he causes sandstorms and tornados as well as rain. Perhaps the most interesting of the Neutral deities is the one with zero adherents, The Nameless. Indeed, no avatar is allowed to follow this deity, who was the ultimate force behind the creation of reality, lacking a distinctive personality, and seeking no personal relationship with living beings.[50]

---

[48] everquest.wikia.com/wiki/Monk

[49] help.daybreakgames.com/hc/en-us/articles/230631567-Marketplace-Race-Change-Scroll-

[50] www.everquest.com/creation

Table 7.5 *The Neutral deities of EverQuest*

Deity	Title	Adherents	Main Races	Main Classes
Karana	The Rain Keeper	3,033	43.2% Halfling 22.6% Half Elf 22.0% Human	52.6% druid 23.8% ranger
Brell Serilis	The Duke of Below	2,589	80.8% Dwarf 14.4% Gnome	38.1% cleric 31.2% paladin 14.6% warrior
The Tribunal	The Council of Justice	2,144	95.6% Barbarian	66.9% shaman 20.0% warrior
Bristlebane	The King of Thieves	1,468	32.2% Halfling 16.6% Wood Elf 16.1% Half Elf	63.2% rogue 17.5% cleric 14.2% bard
Solusek Ro	The Burning Prince	774	27.6% Erudite 26.2% High Elf 15.6% Gnome 15.1% Dark Elf	91.6% wizard
Veeshan	The Mother of all Wurms (dragons)	272	47.4% Drakkin 16.5% Half Elf 12.5% Wood Elf	33.5% bard
Prexus	The Ocean Lord	206	79.1% Erudite	24.8% magician 19.4% enchanter 19.4% paladin 11.7% cleric
The Nameless	None	0	None	None

With only 28.1 percent of the total, the 9,510 adherents of Evil deities are shown in Table 7.6. The situation with Terris-Thule, who has no adherents, is very different from that of The Nameless. A standard part of the *EverQuest* theology is that gods, for a variety of reasons, may abandon their followers and leave the world. Her title, The Dream Scorcher, comes from the fact that she is the origin of nightmares. She can appear temporarily, as an NPC with lines to speak in conversation with other gods and in challenging the player's avatar, notably as one of the opponents in a quest series called Raid Expedition: Plane of Time.[51] Conceivably, in some hypothetical future *EverQuest* expansion, she could return, perhaps as the patron of literal nightmares in some new region, and become a goddess capable of having adherents.

We see that fully 73.1 percent of the followers of Cazic-Thule are Iksar, the reptilian race that has no other choice of deities. However, this does not mean they are monotheists, because they recognize the existence of the deities which other races worship. Necromancers are common among the adherents of Evil gods and are a very interesting class. An *EverQuest* wiki describes this Evil but transcendent profession:

> Necromancers are required to worship an evil god: Bertoxxulous, Innoruuk, or Cazic-Thule, and generally have faction problems in good cities because of this, regardless of race... Necromancers are servants of the dark gods, studying ancient and mysterious tomes to gain power over the dead... Necromancers are able to raise the dead, commanding them to do their bidding and aid them in battle.[52]

To be sure, the *EverQuest* polytheism seems neither realistic to modern secular audiences nor particularly connected to the materialist professions that practice manufacturing. And yet this example suggests a potentially profound insight. If distributed manufacturing erodes globalism, it may result in a proliferation of local cultures, not merely creating household furniture according to local customs, but conceptualizing existence and

---

[51] everquest.allakhazam.com/db/quest.html?quest=4552
[52] everquest.wikia.com/wiki/Necromancer

Table 7.6 *The Evil deities of EverQuest*

Deity	Title	Adherents	Main Races	Main Classes
Cazic-Thule	The Faceless	3,508	73.1% Iksar 14.2% Erudite	32.8% monk 20.3% shadowknight 19.5% necromancer 12.6% shaman
Innoruuk	The Prince of Hate	3,501	82.0% Dark Elf	32.1% necromancer 14.9% cleric
Rallos Zek	The Warlord	1,790	37.0% Ogre 24.5% Barbarian 10.7% Human	74.3% warrior
Bertoxxulous	The Plaguebringer	711	56.3% Gnome 28.4% Human	53.4% necromancer 24.9% shadowknight
Terris-Thule	The Dream Scorcher	0	None	None

morality in distinctive terms. A likely etymology of the word *pagan* is that it represents a locality or a relatively small geographic district, and *paganism* can refer to a religious tradition in which each community has its own spirit or demigod.[53] The pair of *EverQuest* MMOs is by no means the only ones that postulated local religions, *World of Warcraft* being the most influential example. Local communities in a deglobalized era may not go so far as to invent their own religions, but to some degree they are likely to detach from cosmopolitan culture.

Conclusion

Internet-based corporations and professional networks can serve and thereby connect local communities, supporting their independence within a wider technological and economic world. Each MMO has some of the character of a franchise that provides services only to formally regis-tered persons and groups. Thus, the field simulates a future economy that will be highly differentiated yet composed of connections between indi-viduals and corporations at many scales and for many functions. Given the cultural and political diversity the world still possesses, it is entirely likely that manufacture will become local in some areas, whereas other areas perform specialized functions like raw material provision or central-ized mass production. Similarly, we cannot be entirely sure which prod-ucts will be produced locally, although we can guess that really complex products like cars and computers, which require assembly of standardized components manufactured from varied raw materials, will continue to be mass-produced. There is a sense in which the entire computer game industry is a model of the future economy. The games themselves tend to be created by rather small, local companies that may grow if very suc-cessful, be bought up by bigger companies, or use big companies as pub-lishers. The past two decades were a period of radical development in massively multiplayer online games, thus plausibly reflecting any general rules of sociocultural development that apply to the human species, and thereby earning the right to be studied intensively.

---

[53] en.wikipedia.org/wiki/Paganism; en.wikipedia.org/wiki/Pagus

Glossary

Several of these terms have broader meanings outside the massively multiplayer online game industry.

additive manufacture: creation of physical products through progressive application of materials, as, for example, in 3-D printing

avatar: a computer-simulated person that directly represents the user

beta: originally a test version of a computer game through which volunteer players could help designers complete development of the game, but in recent years unfinished games have been more widely distributed, even requiring payment from players

buff: a temporary change to a variable in the algorithm defining a characteristic relevant to the performance of an avatar, such as a food or magic spell that increases the avatar's strength

character: a computer-simulated person that represents a role in a drama, whether operated by a person or automatically

class: a functional category to which an avatar is assigned at the time of creation, for example, a warrior designed for close combat or a healer that helps other avatars during combat

companion: a secondary avatar that accompanies the main avatar of the user, often performing assistive functions

crafting: simulated creation of products from virtual raw materials, requiring possession of particular skills

ethnography: as traditionally defined in cultural anthropology, the documentation of a somewhat coherent native culture through observation and interviews, although in recent years applied in social situations in which a unified and distinctive native culture may not exist

explicit simulation: computer models that represent all the important details of a real-world process

gig economy: a system in which workers are hired temporarily, their work often supported by computer-based technologies

grounded theory: the systematic development of social-scientific theory during research, typically deriving insights from the set of people under study and avoiding preconceptions

guild: a persistent group of avatars within a multiplayer game, usually having its own communication channel and a system of status ranks giving experienced and trusted members more authority

healers: a standard role in combat games, in which an avatar or non-player character cures damage caused by battle wounds

implicit simulation: computer models that represent in detail only some aspects of a real-world process, including other aspects as simple input–output functions

instance: one of two or more similar computer-simulated environments that run separately, for example, one of several identical caverns where multiple teams of players may carry out a particular mission without encountering any other teams that are also doing the mission

leaderboard: a list of avatars in a particular game that ranks them in terms of a particular accomplishment or skill, often placed online and according high social status to the best performers

map: the representation of a bounded physical space inside a computer-based virtual world, whether relatively small like the interior of a building or large like a geographic region.

MMO or MMORPG: a massively multiplayer online role-playing game

mob: contraction of the word "mobile," referring to a simulated person or other agent that can move and act within a computer-simulated environment

mod: contraction of the word "modification," usually referring to an add-on program that can be added to a computer game, or the use of procedures already programmed into the game, to improve performance or transform the game's behavior in a way favorable to the user, but sometimes working against the interests of other players

multiboxing: the use of two or more online game accounts simultaneously, usually on two or more separate computers, running multiple avatars

node: a very specific location in a virtual world where a resource can be harvested

NPC: a nonplayer character, thus a simulated person, animal, or robot that operates independently but interacts with the avatars of human users

participant observation: a sociological method in which a researcher undertakes field research by acting like a nonresearcher who naturally inhabits the intended environment, similar to anthropological ethnography but more experiential

penumbra: the metaphoric shadow cast by an online game, consisting of related forms of social interactions, such as forums, wikis, and social media groups

pet: a secondary avatar usually represented as a tame animal

profession: usually an economic specialty that a player may select for a particular avatar, from a set of other optional specializations

PvE: player-versus-environment, the opposite of PvP, emphasizing collaboration between players whose missions may involve combat with nonplayer characters

PvP: player-versus-player combat in a multiplayer game, emphasized greatly in some games and existing only in certain areas of other games

quest: a mission assigned by the game software to an avatar, with specific goals to be accomplished in a well-defined location

rapid prototyping: an early application for new manufacturing methods, such as 3-D printing, that did not require the lowest cost of production, because the goal was to create an early sample of the product as part of the design process

recipe: sometimes called "schematic" or "book," a simulation of the instructions or computer program for creating a particular product, required before the raw materials can actually be made into the product, often conceptually applied to a simulated manufacturing machine

RPG: a role-playing game which contains a representation of the player as an avatar, usually contrasted with strategy games

RvR: a realm-versus-realm design for conflict between avatar factions, for example, a world in which each of three factions holds its own territory and wars against the other two in contested territories

sandbox: a kind of game that gives players great freedom, for example, allowing them to invest their time in building homes and towns, or exploring the world in whatever way they find interesting, rather than requiring them to accomplish a predetermined set of missions

secondary avatar: the representation of a teammate, assistant, or pet that accompanies and often helps a main avatar

shard: one of several terms describing a separate instantiation of an online game, operated from a dedicated Internet server; shards of the same game may differ by language, rule set, and geographic area

strategy game: a game similar to chess in which each player operates a team of simulated people and that sets a high priority on intellectual analysis of the situation and the best action to take within it

survival game: a game that takes place in a hostile environment where players start with very few resources and must gradually assemble raw materials and construct the equipment necessary to continue exploring the environment

tradeskill: a specialization, such as the crafting of virtual armor or weapons, that has economic value, usually within a game that includes an auction house or other mechanism to support buying and selling between players

virtual world: a persistent, computer-generated representation of a large, diverse physical environment, usually resembling the real world but often containing some mythological elements

wargame: originally intended as a serious training tool for the military, a strategy game that somewhat realistically models real conflict

whale: in "pay-to-win" games, a player who invests excessive amounts of real-world money to gain status

About the Author

William Sims Bainbridge earned a doctorate from Harvard University in sociology and related fields, with a dissertation on the history of the space program, which was published as his first book. Altogether, he has written 30 academic books and about 300 articles or book chapters in areas such as technological innovation, social movements, and modern culture. He has edited two encyclopedias, one on human–computer interaction and the other on leadership in science and technology. He represented the social and information sciences in organizing the Converging Technologies conferences of the U.S. government, which resulted in 11 edited volumes that sought to unite "NBIC:" nanotechnology, biotechnology, information technology and cognitive science. He currently serves as a program director in the Information and Intelligent Systems division of the National Science Foundation.

Index

OTHER TITLES IN OUR COLLABORATIVE INTELLIGENCE COLLECTION

Jim Spohrer, IBM and Haluk Demirkan, Arizona State University, Editors

- *Service Design with Applications to Health Care Institutions* by Oscar Barros
- *How Can Digital Technologies Improve Public Services and Governance?* by Nagy K. Hanna
- *The Accelerating TechnOnomic Medium ('ATOM'): It's Time to Upgrade the Economy* by Kartik Gada
- *Sustainability and the City: The Service Approach* by Adi Wolfson
- *Everything Old is New Again: How Entrepreneurs Use Discourse Themes to Reclaim Abandoned Urban Spaces* by Miriam Plavin-Masterman
- *The Interconnected Individual: Seizing Opportunity in the Era of AI, Platforms, Apps, and Global Exchanges* by Hunter Hastings and Jeff Saperstein
- *T-Shaped Professionals: Adaptive Innovators* by Yassi Moghaddam, Haluk Demirkan, and Jim Spohrer
- *The Value Imperative* by Gautam Mahajan

Announcing the Business Expert Press Digital Library

Concise e-books business students need for classroom and research

This book can also be purchased in an e-book collection by your library as

- a one-time purchase,
- that is owned forever,
- allows for simultaneous readers,
- has no restrictions on printing, and
- can be downloaded as PDFs from within the library community.

Our digital library collections are a great solution to beat the rising cost of textbooks. E-books can be loaded into their course management systems or onto students' e-book readers.
The **Business Expert Press** digital libraries are very affordable, with no obligation to buy in future years. For more information, please visit **www.businessexpertpress.com/librarians**. To set up a trial in the United States, please email **sales@businessexpertpress.com**.

www.ingramcontent.com/pod-product-compliance
Lightning Source LLC
Chambersburg PA
CBHW061212220326
41599CB00025B/4617